Unlocking the Potential of Youth Entrepreneurship in Developing Countries

FROM SUBSISTENCE TO PERFORMANCE

OECD dev

DEVELOPMENT CENTRE

This work is published under the responsibility of the Secretary-General of the OECD. The opinions expressed and arguments employed herein do not necessarily reflect the official views of the member countries of the OECD or its Development Centre.

This document and any map included herein are without prejudice to the status of or sovereignty over any territory, to the delimitation of international frontiers and boundaries and to the name of any territory, city or area.

Please cite this publication as:
OECD (2017), *Unlocking the Potential of Youth Entrepreneurship in Developing Countries: From Subsistence to Performance*, Development Centre Studies, OECD Publishing, Paris.
http://dx.doi.org/10.1787/9789264277830-en

ISBN 978-92-64-27782-3 (print)
ISBN 978-92-64-27783-0 (PDF)

Series: Development Centre Studies
ISSN 1563-4302 (print)
ISSN 1990-0295 (online)

Photo credits: Cover © design by the OECD Development Centre.

Foreword

Demographic pressure and the youth bulge in the developing world pose a major employment challenge, which is exacerbated by insufficient job creation, scarce formal wage employment opportunities and vulnerability in the workplace. This is why fostering youth entrepreneurship has gained importance on the global and national development policy agenda: it is a way to expand employment and earning opportunities for youth. Yet only a tiny portion of youth entrepreneurs in developing countries succeed, while the vast majority are confined to subsistence activities.

This study challenges us to think deeply about how much hope policy makers should place in youth entrepreneurship as a solution to the youth employment challenge. It is intended to sharpen the focus on why a large majority of youth still fail to succeed in entrepreneurship; which policies and programmes can help turn subsistence businesses into productive and performing ones; and which entrepreneurship promotion interventions are more likely to create decent jobs for youth.

This report contributes to the work of the OECD Development Centre on inclusive societies and its objective to help countries identify emerging issues and find innovative solutions to address social challenges and build more cohesive societies. It was undertaken as part of the Youth Inclusion project, co-funded by the European Union and implemented by the OECD Development Centre, to analyse policies for youth and provide evidence for the policy dialogue on youth well-being in developing and emerging countries. It is based on the analysis of quantitative data and the gathering of information on the impact of youth entrepreneurship programmes. The major sources of quantitative data include comparable data from 1-2-3 surveys conducted in Côte d'Ivoire, Madagascar, Peru and Viet Nam. These data have unique advantages for this study: they combine comprehensive information on labour force and enterprises, and they include activities in the predominant unregistered and informal economy. The quantitative analysis was further complemented with information on youth entrepreneurship programmes and existing evidence of the effectiveness of these programmes.

This study adds to the debate on the role of youth entrepreneurship as an engine for decent job creation in developing countries in three important ways. First, it constitutes an unprecedented effort to understand the real situation and the multiple profiles of young entrepreneurs. Second, it provides new empirical evidence on the determinants of youth entrepreneurial performance. Third, it proposes a policy roadmap to help unlock the youth entrepreneurship potential in developing countries.

We hope this study will offer new ideas for bringing policies and programmes in diverse areas together in order to turn subsistence youth businesses into productive and performing ones. Together with the broader set of production transformation, human capital development and employment policies, effective entrepreneurship programmes will bring countries closer to reaching the ambitious targets of full and productive employment and decent work for all, as mandated in Sustainable Development Goal 8.

Mario Pezzini
Director of the Development Centre
and Special Advisor to the OECD Secretary-General on Development

Acknowledgements

The report was prepared by the Social Cohesion Unit of the OECD Development Centre as part of the Youth Inclusion project.

The team was led by Alexandre Kolev, Head of the Social Cohesion Unit and Ji-Yeun Rim, Co-ordinator of the Youth Inclusion project, under the guidance of Mario Pezzini, Director of the OECD Development Centre. The report was drafted by Alexandre Kolev and Pablo Suárez Robles, drawing from a background paper prepared by Axel Demenet, Christophe J. Nordman, Mireille Razafindrakoto and François Roubaud from IRD/DIAL. Mathilde Tarif and Jonathan Broekhuizen provided research assistance.

The report was reviewed by OECD colleagues Stéphane Carcillo (Employment, Labour and Social Affairs), David Halabisky (Centre for Entrepreneurship, SMEs, Local Development and Tourism), Claire Keane (Employment, Labour and Social Affairs), Arthur Minsat (Development Centre), Mariarosa Lunati (Statistics) and Ji-Yeun Rim (Development Centre). It also benefited from valuable inputs and comments from Rolando Avendano (Development Centre), Federico Bonaglia (Development Centre), Lamia Kamal-Chaoui (Centre for Entrepreneurship, SMEs, Local Development and Tourism), Jonathan Potter (Centre for Entrepreneurship, SMEs, Local Development and Tourism), Angel Melguizo (Development Centre), Annalisa Primi (Development Centre), Stefano Scarpetta (Employment, Labour and Social Affairs) and Juan Vazquez Zamora (Development Centre).

Meg Bortin edited the manuscript and Vanda Lintott oversaw the production of the publication.

The Youth Inclusion project is co-financed by the European Union.

Table of contents

Tables

For many young people in the developing world, entrepreneurial activity is the sole entry point into the labour market and the only way out of poverty. Yet only a tiny portion of youth entrepreneurs record high performance in terms of profits and job creation. In this context, how much hope should policy makers place on entrepreneurship programmes as a solution to the youth employment challenge in developing countries?

The main objective of this study is to contribute to the ongoing debate on the role of youth entrepreneurship in generating employment in developing countries. It prompts a series of questions that are crucial to helping policy makers leverage the youth entrepreneurship potential for decent job creation: How many youth are entrepreneurs? What are the characteristics of their businesses? How do they perform? What factors drive performance or failure? How successful are interventions that aim to promote youth entrepreneurship? Which design features can enhance the effectiveness of entrepreneurship programme?

This report is based on the analysis of mixed labour force and enterprise surveys conducted in Côte d'Ivoire, Madagascar, Peru and Viet Nam, as well as the gathering of evidence on the impact of entrepreneurship programmes in developing countries. This report adds to the global debate on youth entrepreneurship in three important ways.

First, it constitutes an unprecedented effort to capture the real situation and multiple faces of young entrepreneurs in four developing countries – Côte d'Ivoire, Madagascar, Peru and Viet Nam – that represent a rather diverse set of conditions in terms of geographical location and income level. The study shows that many young people engage in entrepreneurship for lack of a better job. The majority of youth entrepreneurs operate as small informal businesses in petty trade and services and few possess basic business skills. By and large, youth entrepreneurship is less financially rewarding than wage employment. Only a tiny proportion of youth entrepreneurs can be considered top performers, generating both high profits and jobs.

Second, it provides new empirical evidence on the determinants of youth entrepreneurial performance. It shows that education, managerial capital and business skills are key factors for success. At the same time, young women and rural dwellers face particular disadvantage. While the quality of the business environment varies significantly across countries, informality is common everywhere and unambiguously drives youth business performance down. The vast majority of businesses operate on the streets or at home, with only very few having dedicated premises. Favourable operating conditions often lead to higher youth entrepreneurial performance. Finally, access to finance and market integration present major challenges.

Third, it proposes a policy roadmap based on lessons learned from recent meta-analysis of the effectiveness of entrepreneurship programmes. Unlocking the youth entrepreneurship potential in developing countries calls for a number of actions at programme and policy levels.

At programme level:

- design interventions that are carefully targeted and tailored to address specific challenges and needs of young entrepreneurs, a highly heterogeneous group;
- link the design of youth entrepreneurship programmes with impact evaluation results;
- invest in comprehensive entrepreneurship programmes;
- reallocate resources away from ineffective programmes.

At policy level:

- integrate entrepreneurship education in formal schooling;
- promote youth entrepreneurship spirit through success stories and role models;
- simplify administrative procedures;
- encourage formalisation as a way to support business expansion;
- develop a holistic and long-term vision in order to foster local and global value chain development.

The report is structured as follows. Chapter 1 considers the meaning of youth entrepreneurship in the context of developing countries. Chapter 2 provides a detailed portrait of youth entrepreneurs in Côte d'Ivoire, Madagascar, Peru and Viet Nam. Chapter 3 discusses pathways and barriers to youth entrepreneurship performance in these four countries. Chapter 4 concludes the report by proposing some policy directions.

Assessment and recommendations

As many as 600 million jobs will need to be created worldwide over the next 15 years to keep employment rates at their current level. The employment challenge is particularly pressing in developing countries, where demographic pressures are often stronger, wage employment opportunities are scarce and formal job creation is insufficient to give most youth access to decent work. In this context, fostering youth entrepreneurship has gained importance on the global and national policy agendas as a way to expand employment and earning opportunities.

Only a tiny portion of youth entrepreneurs prove to be successful, however, and a large number are confined to subsistence activities, especially in developing countries. This study focuses on four countries – Côte d'Ivoire, Madagascar, Peru and Viet Nam – where the vast majority of young entrepreneurs, from 57% in Viet Nam to 86% in Côte d'Ivoire, record profits below the average wage earned by young employees. The fact that a large majority of youth are still failing to succeed as entrepreneurs casts doubts on how much hope policy makers can place on youth entrepreneurship as a solution to the youth employment challenge.

This study argues that greater attention to these issues is needed in order to unlock the youth entrepreneurship potential in developing countries. While a small portion of youth entrepreneurs can benefit from specific policies and programmes to make profits and scale up their businesses, a majority of youth in subsistence activities will need to transition into the labour market with the support of policies that focus on improving skills and employability. The study looks at which policies and programmes can help certain youth profiles to turn their activities into more productive and performing ones, and which types of entrepreneurship promotion intervention are more likely to create decent jobs for youth.

Using micro data from Côte d'Ivoire, Madagascar, Peru and Viet Nam, and recent meta-analysis on the effectiveness of entrepreneurship programmes in developing countries, this study prompts a series of questions that are crucial to helping policy makers leverage the youth entrepreneurship potential for decent job creation: How many youth are opportunity-driven entrepreneurs? What are the characteristics of their businesses? How do they perform? What factors drive performance or failure? How successful are interventions that aim to promote youth entrepreneurship? Which design features can enhance entrepreneurship programme effectiveness?

Understanding youth entrepreneurship

Youth entrepreneurship can be defined as self-employment among youth. There is no internationally agreed definition of entrepreneurship due to the complexity of the notion and its multifaceted nature. This leaves room for a multiplicity of definitions. Following standard practice for developing countries, this study will use self-employment as a proxy for entrepreneurship in both the formal and informal sectors, and will use the age range 15-29 to define a youth entrepreneur. The concept of entrepreneurship encompasses a very heterogeneous reality that can be seen as a continuum of businesses operating at different performance levels, ranging from own-account workers and micro-enterprises to large companies; from necessity-driven, subsistence and informal businesses to opportunity-driven, highly profitable and innovative formal enterprises; from businesses relying on informal networks to enterprises well-connected to local and global value chains and markets.

Measuring youth entrepreneurship and entrepreneurial performance is challenging in the developing world. The data used to analyse entrepreneurship in advanced economies are not suitable for developing countries. In developing countries, informality is the norm, and therefore businesses that operate in the informal sector must be included. While data gaps and limitations make it difficult to obtain representative and reliable quantitative information on entrepreneurship in developing countries, a number of surveys, with varying levels of representativeness and detail, can be used to measure entrepreneurship. This study adopts an innovative approach by using data from linked labour force and enterprise surveys for Côte d'Ivoire, Madagascar, Peru and Viet Nam. While these linked surveys, also called 1-2-3 surveys, are not exempt from certain limitations, they are optimal for analysing youth entrepreneurship. This is because they are nationally representative, cross-country comparable and include businesses operating in the informal sector. Measuring success further adds to our understanding of entrepreneurship. Yet it brings an additional layer of complexity, as there is no one single indicator that can adequately assess the multifaceted aspects of entrepreneurial performance. Use of a comprehensive set of indicators is often recommended, such as those proposed in the OECD-Eurostat Entrepreneurship Indicators Programme (EIP). For data availability reasons and given their importance, profitability and job creation are the two main indicators of entrepreneurial performance used in this report. These two outcomes are fundamental for measuring entrepreneurial performance. Profits are measured through information on sales and expenditures. Job creation is measured by considering both business employment size growth and propensity to offer jobs to external wage workers. Depending on their level of profits and job creation, youth businesses are then classified as top performers, mid performers and low performers.

Portraits of youth entrepreneurs

Many young people engage in entrepreneurship. Although it is not the dominant form of youth employment, youth entrepreneurship is a significant phenomenon. It is defined here as comprising all non-farm household unincorporated businesses operated by youth, either as own-account workers or employers. The majority of young entrepreneurs work in rural non-farm businesses, and most are poorly educated. Youth entrepreneurs from Côte d'Ivoire, Madagascar, Peru and Viet Nam operate in rather different conditions that mirror the diversity of the developing world, in terms of both geographical location and income level. The extent of youth entrepreneurship as the main occupation varies greatly across countries, ranging from 14% in Viet Nam to 43.9% in Côte d'Ivoire of the total youth employed (outside agriculture). The vast majority of entrepreneurs, in particular youth, are own-account workers. And while youth-run businesses account for a non-negligible share of all businesses, a number of these are operated as a secondary occupation. Interestingly, there seems to be a generational transition towards wage employment as countries develop economically.

Young people often appear to go into business for lack of a better job. A large majority of youth from Côte d'Ivoire, Madagascar, Peru and Viet Nam declare that they are running a business by choice and appear rather optimistic about the future. Yet, looking deeper, underemployment and multiple job holding are more prevalent among these youth entrepreneurs than among youth employees, revealing that youth entrepreneurship is most likely driven by necessity, notably due to the lack of wage employment opportunities. The youth employment challenge is thus primarily structural and driven by insufficient aggregate labour demand. The lack of wage employment opportunities for youth, which forces many of them to enter entrepreneurship, is probably a leading cause of youth business failure in developing settings. Motivation for running a business is also influenced by culture and societal values, which shape attitudes towards entrepreneurship.

Few youth entrepreneurs possess basic business skills. Information shows that very few young entrepreneurs use written accounts. Available data from Madagascar highlight the lack of business practices among young entrepreneurs. Youth businesses are typically very small. They primarily operate in petty trade and services, often referred to as free-entry sectors, and almost all of them are unregistered with the authorities.

Youth entrepreneurship is less financially rewarding than wage employment. Although the vast majority of young entrepreneurs generate profits, these are most often modest and below the level of income earned by youth in wage employment. The distribution of profits is more unequal than in the more advanced countries. Relatively few youth businesses generate employment. When youth entrepreneurs recruit, they rely almost exclusively on family members. Only a tiny proportion of youth entrepreneurs can be considered top performers who generate both high profits and jobs.

Pathways and barriers to performance

Education significantly increases youth entrepreneurial performance. Managerial capital and business skills are also key for success. Cross- and within-country econometric analyses show that entrepreneurial performance is driven by multiple factors. Two groups in particular face disadvantages in terms of business performance: young women and rural dwellers.

Informality weakens youth business performance. While the quality of the business environment varies significantly across countries, informality is common everywhere and unambiguously drives youth business performance down. Depending on the country, reasons for being informal range from tax avoidance to the high cost of registration or simply a lack of information. There is also evidence that the sector of activity affects performance, although this varies across countries. For instance, in more economically advanced developing settings, manufacturing seems to offer the highest chances for youth to move up the entrepreneurial performance ladder.

Favourable physical operating conditions raise performance. The vast majority of businesses operate on the streets or at home. Only very few have dedicated premises. Favourable operating conditions – such as access to dedicated premises, basic infrastructure services and information and communication technologies (ICT) – often lead to higher youth entrepreneurial performance. Yet few businesses have access to basic infrastructure services (water and electricity) and, in particular, to ICT (phone and, to a larger extent, Internet).

Access to finance and market integration present major challenges. Access to credit is a primary concern for a large number of youth businesses. Youth have to deal with a lack of personal savings and resources; inadequate youth-friendly financial products, including micro-lending and seed funding; high credit and collateral requirements, and excessive restrictions (e.g. age limit to open a bank account); low financial literacy; and limited knowledge of financing opportunities. The fact that youth businesses are poorly integrated into markets is another barrier to performance. Youth businesses rarely interact with larger private companies, and in particular with the public sector. By and large, they buy and sell products or services to individuals and other small businesses.

The way forward: Helping youth entrepreneurs reach their potential

Unlocking the youth entrepreneurship potential in developing countries calls for a number of actions at programme and policy levels.

At programme level:

Design interventions that are carefully targeted and tailored to address specific challenges and needs of young entrepreneurs, a highly heterogeneous group. Young entrepreneurs in developing countries face tremendous constraints that confine a large number of them to subsistence activities. Only a tiny number of young entrepreneurs prove to be successful, demonstrating that moving up the entrepreneurial performance ladder is difficult but not impossible. Evidence on enabling and disabling factors for higher entrepreneurial performance highlights the need to invest on multiple and concomitant fronts, through a comprehensive approach. The high heterogeneity observed among youth entrepreneurs calls for policy solutions and interventions that should be carefully targeted to profiles with real entrepreneurial potential, while those engaged in subsistence activities should be trained and redirected to transition into the labour market or public works programmes.

- **Link the design of youth entrepreneurship programmes with impact evaluation results**. Improving business performance and enhancing employment creation is complex. There is little evidence on the impact of entrepreneurship programmes, in particular for youth, but some studies have tried to estimate causal impacts of an intervention using randomised controlled trials or quasi-experimental techniques. Findings show that few programmes have been able to create employment in already existing firms. Moreover, programme effectiveness varies across interventions. While business development services appear to contribute effectively to business expansion, other programmes have been less successful. Financial interventions seem to be more effective in establishing new firms than in contributing to business expansion or increased employment. Entrepreneurship training programmes appear able to improve business skills but their impact on job creation is mixed. By the same token, interventions promoting formalisation tend to yield insignificant or modest positive employment effects, mainly because most informal businesses are too small and not profitable enough to take advantage of the potential benefits of formality.

- **Invest in comprehensive entrepreneurship programmes**. An important lesson from impact evaluation is that adopting a comprehensive, integrated approach is important, since stand-alone programmes are generally found to be less effective. Entrepreneurship programmes are indeed more successful when they provide comprehensive packages offering multiple services simultaneously. It is also important that programmes be country specific, adapted to local contexts and tailored to the needs of entrepreneurs that may have different potentials.

- **Reallocate resources away from ineffective programmes**. Resources must be reallocated away from ineffective programmes and towards the most promising interventions. Business development services have an established track record of contributing effectively to business performance and employment generation, and there is a strong case for supporting them. Adequate resources are needed to ensure that business assistance and support services are available in the medium to long term. While medium- to long-term assistance is key to raising survival rates, business development services are too often short term, and assistance rarely extends beyond the first year of business operation. Moreover, given the importance of favourable physical operating conditions in driving up youth entrepreneurship performance, investment in this area holds great promise. Examples include investing in business incubators, creating shared working hubs, providing or sharing basic service equipment and creating business network platforms.

At policy level:

- **Integrate entrepreneurship education in formal schooling**. Education policy and the formal schooling system must integrate comprehensive entrepreneurship education into the national curriculum at all levels. Comprehensive curricula need to be developed to provide young people with different sets of competencies, including technical, non-cognitive and life skills as well as entrepreneurial behaviour. More attention should also be paid to business development skills and real-world knowledge in vocational training.

- **Promote youth entrepreneurship spirit through success stories and role models**. The talent of young entrepreneurs should be highlighted by organising conferences and highly visible summits, and by supporting youth entrepreneurship competitions, awards and events to raise the profile of young entrepreneurs and create awareness about entrepreneurship. The development of networks of young entrepreneurs must be encouraged through peer networks grouping youth entrepreneurship organisations, business associations, youth-led organisations and other stakeholders. Entrepreneurship potential can also be promoted via knowledge exchange between established businesses and aspiring young entrepreneurs. Ultimately, young entrepreneurs must be given more visibility. To this end, media and other communication tools and platforms can be used, in particular to promote role models.

- **Simplify administrative procedures**. This can be achieved by making business registration quicker and less expensive, simplifying tax filing requirements and accounting methods, and reviewing bankruptcy laws to make them more tolerant of risk taking and business failure. Tax regimes must be rendered more supportive, for instance by lowering tax rates or introducing tax and social contribution exemptions for young entrepreneurs. In addition, the business regulatory environment needs to be more predictable.

- **Encourage formalisation as a way to support business expansion**. A right mix of incentives and sanctions is needed to encourage formalisation. Formalisation benefits businesses by changing their operating conditions. Released from the constraints of informality, they can access better equipment, increase their scale of operation and operate in a more competitive environment. However, not all enterprises benefit in the same way, and among the smallest and most precarious production units, the effect of formalisation is still unclear. Rather than strict enforcement of formality, which is often socially costly and rarely efficient, the way to go is probably to encourage registration, especially through fiscal incentives, awareness-raising campaigns, simplification of business regulations, and business advice and training for informal entrepreneurs. Along these lines, there is also a need to reduce the incentives for remaining informal. This demands careful monitoring of the impact of taxes and social contributions.

- **Develop a holistic and long-term vision in order to foster local and global value chain development**. Although evidence is still scarce on the impact of value chain interventions, fostering integration into local and global value chains can potentially have a large impact on employment creation and job quality. One important area of action at the national level is to link entrepreneurs to multinational enterprises and global value chains by attracting foreign direct investment and promoting supplier development. At the sub-national level, greater emphasis should be devoted to supporting local value chains by improving the functioning and the integration of local markets.

Chapter 1

Understanding youth entrepreneurship

Defining and measuring youth entrepreneurship is complex. There is no internationally agreed definition of youth entrepreneurship, and data gaps make it difficult to obtain reliable information on youth entrepreneurs in developing countries. This chapter focuses on definition and measurement issues and their importance for our understanding of youth entrepreneurship. In particular, it presents the operational definitions and survey data used for the empirical analysis conducted in four selected developing countries: Côte d'Ivoire, Madagascar, Peru and Viet Nam.

In low- and middle-income countries, self-employment is the dominant form of entrepreneurship and accounts for an important share of youth employment. According to the Global Entrepreneurship Monitor (GEM), a significant proportion of the youth population aged 18 to 24 were nascent entrepreneurs or owners-managers of a new business in 2016 – about 10% in Asia and Oceania, 15% in Africa and 17% in Latin America and the Caribbean (Keller, Singer and Herrington, 2016). For many people in these regions, including youth, entrepreneurial activity is the sole entry point into the labour market and the only way out of poverty. In sub-Saharan Africa, for example, approximately one-third of all youth with a new or nascent business were pushed towards entrepreneurship out of necessity (Kew, 2015; YBI, 2013). Often this involved small-scale self-employed subsistence activities, in farming or outside the agricultural sector (Margolis, 2014).

Yet at the other end of the spectrum, a tiny portion of entrepreneurs record high performance levels in terms of profits, employment generation, productivity or other factors. Evidence shows that those who opt voluntarily for entrepreneurship tend to take advantage of market opportunities and start their own business even though they could generate income through other forms of employment (YBI, 2012). In particular, youth who are entrepreneurs out of vocation tend to have the ability to identify good business opportunities and possess better skills to start up a new business and make it grow. These young entrepreneurs constitute a small group, however. Could entrepreneurship be a solution to the youth employment challenge in developing countries?

Youth entrepreneurship can be defined as self-employment among youth

There is no internationally agreed definition of entrepreneurship. This has left room for a multiplicity of diverging definitions. Attempts to define the concept of entrepreneurship date back to the 18th century and have concerned many fields of study, including psychology, sociology, economics and management (Congregado, 2008). The complexity of the notion of entrepreneurship and its multifaceted nature make the development of a standard definition a difficult exercise. In recent years, international organisations have proposed a number of definitions (Rabboir [1995, as quoted in Chigunta, 2002] already listed twenty definitions of entrepreneurship two decades ago) without agreeing on a unified understanding of the concept (Box 1.1). The OECD-Eurostat Entrepreneurship Indicators Programme (EIP) in 2016 became the first international programme to provide a structured conceptual framework for the measurement of the multiple dimensions of entrepreneurship, including its determinants, performance outcomes and impacts on the economy (OECD, 2016). International definitions do share some notions, such as risk taking, creativity and innovation. However, these underlying notions are generally too abstract and theoretical for definitions of entrepreneurship to be operational from a statistical point of view. This is why, in practice, self-employment and entrepreneurship are often interchangeably used.

This report uses self-employment as a proxy for entrepreneurship. Self-employment is widely used as a proxy of entrepreneurship in developed and developing countries. All self-employed workers face risks, seek to transform their labour input into profits and earn an income through the value-added of their business. As such, they can all be considered entrepreneurs in a broad sense. Self-employment encompasses many forms of work. When used as a proxy of entrepreneurship, self-employment is usually restricted to own-account workers and employers, leaving aside particular employment statuses such as contributing family workers and members of producers' cooperatives. Such exclusion is justified by the fact that the work performed under such statuses is quite distant from the common understanding and positive connotations associated with entrepreneurship. Self-employment data used in this report encompass most entrepreneurs, including the so-called "missing" entrepreneurs who operate in the informal sector (OECD/EU, 2015). However, the data do not cover people running incorporated businesses, whose relative number is usually very low in developing countries, nor do they include individuals who are in the process of setting up a business but have not yet realised its creation. Analysing these particular categories of entrepreneurs is beyond the scope of this study and requires alternative data such as those provided by the Global Entrepreneurship Monitor (GEM).

This report uses the age range 15-29 to define a youth entrepreneur. Official definitions of the youth population diverge across the four countries. Youth are defined at the national level as all individuals aged 16-35 in Côte d'Ivoire (2016-2020 National Youth Policy), aged 14-35 in Madagascar (2004 National Youth Policy), aged 15-29 in Peru (2012 National Youth Strategy) and aged 16-30 in Viet Nam (Youth Law and 2011 Youth Development Strategy). Yet a common definition is needed across the four countries for the sake of comparability. The United Nations, for statistical purposes, defines youth as people between the ages of 15 and 24 (UN DESA, 2010). This age range is too restrictive when analysing youth employment for several reasons. First, as put forward by ILO (2015b), increasing the upper age limit makes sense and is actually receiving growing attention since educational attainment is increasing worldwide and youth tend more and more to postpone labour market entry beyond the age of 24. Second, the choice of a restrictive upper boundary tends to bias the population under study towards less educated young workers and to deflate the extent of youth entrepreneurship. Third, from a purely statistical point of view, extending the upper age limit increases the number of observations and thus offers more in-depth analytical possibilities.

Entrepreneurship is a dynamic process that can encompass many goals. The situation of entrepreneurs is not static but changes over time, with businesses going through different phases. For instance, GEM (Kelley et al., 2016) proposes a business life-cycle model that includes four successive phases: conception (potential and nascent entrepreneurs); birth and early stage (new businesses); persistence (established businesses); and discontinuance (business conclusion). Entrepreneurship also encompasses many types of businesses that differ in terms of purpose, goals or organisational form. Most entrepreneurs seek wealth creation and profit generation (economic entrepreneurship), but others, who are increasing in number worldwide, aim to create social value beyond pursuing financial self-sustainability (social entrepreneurship) (ILO, 2006). Moreover, empirical evidence in developing countries on the dynamic nature of entrepreneurship and the different types of business is very scarce, if not inexistent.

Entrepreneurship is a continuum of businesses operating at different performance levels. This continuum is highly heterogeneous. It ranges from own-account workers and microenterprises to large companies; from necessity driven, subsistence and informal businesses to opportunity driven, highly profitable and innovative formal enterprises; from businesses relying on informal networks to enterprises well connected to local and global value chains and markets.

Box 1.1. **How different international organisations define entrepreneurship**

- **OECD-Eurostat**: Entrepreneurship is defined by the OECD-Eurostat Entrepreneurship Indicators Programme (EIP) as the "phenomenon associated with entrepreneurial activity, which is the enterprising human action in pursuit of the generation of value, through the creation or expansion of economic activity, by identifying and exploiting new products, processes or markets" (Ahmad and Seymour, 2008). This is the first international programme to provide a structured conceptual framework for the measurement of entrepreneurship. The EIP framework proposes three sets of indicators measuring: i) the determinants of entrepreneurship; ii) entrepreneurial performance; and iii) the impacts of entrepreneurship on the economy. At present, the EIP remains the only articulated international initiative aimed at assisting in and providing guidance on the measurement of all the different dimensions of entrepreneurship.

> Box 1.1. **How different international organisations define entrepreneurship** *(cont.)*
>
> * **Global Entrepreneurship Monitor:** Entrepreneurship is defined as "any attempt at new business or new venture creation, such as self-employment, a new business organisation or the expansion of an existing business, by an individual, a team of individuals, or an established business" (http://www.gemconsortium.org/wiki/1149).
> * **European Commission:** Entrepreneurship is defined as "an individual's ability to turn ideas into action. It includes creativity, innovation, risk taking, ability to plan and manage projects in order to achieve objectives". (https://ec.europa.eu/growth/smes/promoting-entrepreneurship_fr)
> * **ILO:** Entrepreneurship is the "recognition of an opportunity to create value, and the process of acting on this opportunity, whether or not it involves the formation of a new entity. While concepts such as innovation and risk taking in particular are usually associated with entrepreneurship, they are not necessary to define the term." (ILO, 2006)

Measuring youth entrepreneurship is challenging in the developing world

Data sources used in advanced economies are not suitable for developing countries. Measurement data used in advanced economies typically combine information from business registers, tax sources and enterprise surveys produced by well-established national statistical offices and administrative records. These data sources are generally of good quality, available on a frequent basis and comprehensive enough to cover the whole spectrum of enterprises, including the smallest ones. They do not (or rarely) take account of businesses that operate in the informal sector or engage in illegal activities. In advanced economies, this number is quite low, accounting for a marginal share of existing enterprises. The situation is radically different in developing countries, where informality is the norm, not the exception (Jutting and de Laiglesia, 2009). Drawing on business registers or other official data sources in these countries would result in a partial and biased picture of entrepreneurship, given that only a tiny portion of businesses, and mainly just the largest companies, are registered with the authorities.

Data gaps make it difficult to obtain representative and reliable information. Despite recent progress, basic labour market indicators on entrepreneurship are lacking or incomplete in many developing countries. Limitations are far worse when it comes to enterprise-level data on self-employed workers: statistics on the predominant and massive unregistered sector are, for obvious reasons, difficult to produce. However, there exist a number of surveys, with varying levels of representativeness and detail that can be used to get a sense of entrepreneurship (Box 1.2).

> Box 1.2. **How different surveys analyse entrepreneurship**
>
> * **Enterprise surveys:** Traditionally the main source of information for analysing production units, these surveys are designed to measure inputs, outputs and main characteristics. They are of limited relevance in developing countries, however, because samples are usually based on registered businesses and thus pose major coverage and bias problems.
> * **Living standards and measurement surveys:** Primarily aimed at measuring consumption and poverty, these surveys also collect a large variety of well-being indicators on areas such as employment, education, health, fertility, nutrition and housing conditions. However, information on employment is often limited and based on short reference periods. This is problematic when analysing rural employment in particular, given the seasonal nature of agricultural activities.

> **Box 1.2. How different surveys analyse entrepreneurship** *(cont.)*
>
> - **Labour force surveys**: Unanimously considered the best survey instrument for deriving employment and labour market indicators, these surveys are drawn from censuses. They usually have large coverage and a high level of representativeness, and contain rich information on work-related activities. But unless specific modules are included, information on self-employment characteristics and outcomes generally lacks precision.
> - **Global Entrepreneurship Monitor surveys**: These household surveys are widely used to measure entrepreneurship activities and attitudes. They can identify entrepreneurs at different stages of the business life cycle, including nascent entrepreneurs in the process of setting up a business who have not yet realised its creation. However, information on the quality of entrepreneurship is rather limited compared to alternative data sources.
> - **Linked labour force-enterprise surveys**: This approach has the advantage of combining the large coverage of labour force surveys with the high level of detail of enterprise surveys, thereby providing an optimal source of information for analysing entrepreneurship.

This report adopts an innovative approach for measuring entrepreneurship. It uses raw data from linked labour force and enterprise surveys for Côte d'Ivoire, Madagascar, Peru and Viet Nam. These linked surveys, also called 1-2-3 surveys, are optimal for analysing entrepreneurship in that they combine the large coverage of labour force surveys with the high level of detail of enterprise surveys. Their principle is to build a comprehensive listing of businesses through a first-phase household survey on employment, which resembles a traditional labour force survey thanks to specific filter questions identifying own-account workers and employers. The sample of businesses extracted from the first phase is then used to conduct a second-phase enterprise-type survey (Box 1.3). In this report, the first phase is used to identify entrepreneurs and document their main individual, household and job characteristics. The second phase is used to analyse business characteristics as well as entrepreneurial behaviours and perceptions of the entrepreneurs identified in the first phase. The third phase, which is not used in this report, focuses on household consumption expenditure and allows analysis of poverty.

Using linked surveys has several advantages. It overcomes the lack of coverage of alternative data sources by taking account unregistered businesses. In addition, it allows representativeness at the national level by covering both urban and rural areas; such coverage is often lacking in data from developing countries. First conducted in Cameroon in 1993, 1-2-3 surveys have since been replicated in many countries across Latin America, Africa and Asia. These linked surveys are carried out by national statistical institutes with technical support from IRD/DIAL. Their richness lies in their cross-country comparability, their high representativeness with the inclusion of the informal sector and their detailed information at the production unit level.

These linked surveys are not exempt from certain limitations. First, they only account for household unincorporated businesses. Second, and more importantly, these surveys focus exclusively on non-agricultural activities. Unincorporated businesses are enterprises owned by individuals or households that are not constituted as separate legal entities independently of their owners. These surveys are not designed to capture household businesses that are incorporated. However, the omission of this category, while constituting a clear data limitation, should not pose a major problem since their relative number is usually very low in developing countries. It is, however, problematic that enterprises operating in the farming sector are not taken into account because the countries under study are still predominantly agrarian and thus are composed of a large share of farmers. Nonetheless, from an economic point of view, there is a rationale for restricting the analysis to the non-agricultural sector because the deeply rooted structural differences between farm and non-farm activities make them hardly comparable. Moreover, to properly take account of agricultural production and activities, adapted survey methodologies and instruments would be needed to reflect their specificities in terms of seasonality, labour organisation, capital and income. Exclusion of agriculture is actually quite common and even recommended under international guidelines in OECD and EU countries (OECD, 2015; EUROSTAT-OECD, 2007).

Box 1.3. **The surveys used in this report**

- **Côte d'Ivoire:** We used the 2014 *Enquête Nationale sur l'Emploi et le Travail des Enfants* (ENSETE), which surveyed 12 000 households nationwide. There is no Phase 2, but instead a specific module on non-farm businesses integrated into the household survey. The level of detail is consequently lower, but comparability with other countries remains high since Ivoirian and Peruvian data are based on the same scheme as the 1-2-3 surveys and thus share many common points.

- **Madagascar:** We used Phases 1 and 2 of the 2012 *Enquête Nationale sur l'Emploi et le Secteur Informel* (ENEMPSI). The first phase surveyed 11 300 households and the second included all identified production units, 5 700 in total. This survey was the first of its kind conducted in the country, and as such provided the first estimates of the number of non-agricultural production units.

- **Peru:** We used the annual 2014 *Encuesta Nacional de Hogares* (ENAHO). This is a continuous survey with annual data comprising 40 125 households. Instead of a separate second phase, the ENAHO incorporates a specific module on self-employment and non-agricultural production. ENAHO data are renowned for their high quality.

- **Viet Nam:** For Phase 1, we used the annual 2014 *Labour Force Survey* (LFS), which is conducted quarterly, using a rotating panel. In 2014 it included 50 640 households per quarter, equivalent to 16 880 households per month. Phase 2 draws on the *Household Business and Informal Sector Survey* (HBIS) conducted in 2014 among 3 411 businesses extracted from the LFS.

No single indicator can adequately assess entrepreneurial performance. Use of a comprehensive set of indicators is often recommended, such as those proposed in the OECD-Eurostat EIP framework. This framework revolves around three different levels: firm-based, employment-based and wealth performance (OECD, 2016). From a micro perspective, performance indicators usually focus on business survival, employment size and growth, earnings, profits, value-added, productivity, innovation and so on. Beyond purely economic and enterprise-wide outcomes, other achievements in the social and environmental spheres are just as valuable for characterising entrepreneurial performance, if not more so. The social economy is increasingly demonstrating in practice that entrepreneurial behaviour is not antagonistic to meeting social needs and serving the general interest and common good for the benefit of the community. On the contrary, social enterprises play an essential role in addressing social, economic and environmental challenges, and in fostering inclusive growth, enhancing local social capital, and contributing to social inclusion by delivering good quality welfare services (OECD, 2013).

Profitability and job creation are the main indicators of performance used in this report. These two outcomes are fundamental for measuring entrepreneurial performance, especially in the context of developing countries. While profits capture the main monetary outcome of business performance, employment creation is all the more socially valuable, in particular when job opportunities are offered to external workers and not only to family members or people in immediate social networks who can lack the qualifications needed.

Information on sales and expenditures are used to measure profits. Measuring profits in developing countries is often a challenge since many businesses do not possess written accounts. The linked labour force-enterprise surveys used in this report overcome the challenge of measuring profits by asking surveyed business owners for their complete list of sales and expenditures during a reference period (except in Côte d'Ivoire where respondents were asked to self-report their profits). With such detailed information on flows of outputs and inputs related to all goods and services produced and used, it is possible to obtain estimates of profits for all businesses, regardless of whether they keep accounts. There has been debate recently on the relevance of such detailed questionnaires used in this measurement method over direct self-reporting. According to de Mel et al. (2009), self-reporting provides a more accurate measure of profits than questions on revenues and expenses. However, despite its potential for underreporting and recall biases, the rigorous methodology used in these linked surveys has proved to produce more reliable and stable measurement of profits. In fact, information obtained with this methodology is generally of higher comparability across surveyed production units and less subject to measurement errors (ILO, 2013; ADB, 2011). In the empirical analysis, profits are annualised, adjusted for seasonality and converted to US dollars at purchasing power parity (PPP) to allow cross-country comparability.

Two considerations are used to measure job creation. The first, business employment size growth, is simply measured as the difference between initial employment size upon business creation and current size (data not available for Peru). The second, the propensity to offer jobs to external wage workers, corresponds to the presence of employees recruited outside the family nucleus. These indicators complement the income-generating capacity of businesses as measured through profits by indicating whether young entrepreneurs, who for the vast majority set up their business alone, are able to grow, create jobs and recruit external employees. The comparative job creation potential of micro and small versus large enterprises is a question debated in the empirical literature. Micro and small enterprises dominate the share of existing employment, but their contribution to net job creation is harder to evidence. This question concerns youth in the first place since, as seen in advanced economies, young enterprises appear to be responsible for a large proportion of job creation and destruction in the economy (OECD, 2010).

Profits and job creation are used to classify youth business performers. Low performers comprise youth businesses with the lowest profits (bottom tertile of the distribution of profits). Mid performers include youth businesses with intermediate levels of profits (second tertile), as well as youth businesses with the highest profits (top tertile) that did not grow in employment size since their creation (for Peru, since information on initial employment size is missing, the job creation criterion is replaced by the presence of external wage workers). Finally, top performers comprise youth businesses that generated the highest profits (top tertile) and also created jobs. This classification provides a simple and innovative approach that combines two major performance outcomes and that clearly defines and differentiates three gradual steps of the entrepreneurial performance ladder.

References

Asian Development Bank (2011), *A handbook on using the mixed survey for measuring informal employment and the informal sector*, ADB, Mandaluyong City, Philippines.

Ahmad, N. & Seymour, R. G. (2008), "Defining Entrepreneurial Activity: Definitions Supporting Frameworks for Data Collection", *OECD Statistics Working Paper*, STD/DOC(2008)1, OECD Publishing, Paris, http://dx.doi.org/ 10.1787/243164686763.

Chigunta, F. (2002), "Youth entrepreneurship: Meeting the key policy challenges" (online draft).

Congregado, E. (ed.) (2008), *Measuring Entrepreneurship: Building a Statistical System*, Springer Science and Business Media, LLC, New York.

International Labour Office, (2013), *Measuring Informality: A Statistical Manual on the Informal Sector and Informal Employment*, ILO, Geneva.

International Labour Organization (2006), *Stimulating Youth Entrepreneurship: Barriers and Incentives to Enterprise Start-Ups by Young People*, ILO, Geneva.

Jütting, J. and J.R. de Laiglesia, (eds.) (2009), *Is informal Normal? Towards More and Better Jobs in Developing Countries*, OECD Development Centre, OECD Publishing, Paris.

Kelley, D., S. Singer and M. Herrington (2016). "Global entrepreneurship monitor: 2015/16 global report", Global Entrepreneurship Research Association, London Business School.

Kew, J. (2015), *Africa's Young Entrepreneurs: Unlocking the Potential for a Brighter Future*, Rothko, Cape Town.

Margolis, D.N. (2014). "By choice and by necessity: Entrepreneurship and self-employment in the developing world", in *European Journal of Development Research*, Vol. 26/4, pp. 419–436, Springer.

OECD (2016), *Entrepreneurship at a Glance 2016*, OECD Publishing, Paris. http://dx.doi.org/10.1787/entrepreneur_aag-2016-en

OECD (2015), *Entrepreneurship at a Glance 2015*, OECD Publishing, Paris, http://dx.doi.org/10.1787/entrepreneur_aag-2015-en.

OECD (2013), *Policy Brief on Social Entrepreneurship: Entrepreneurial Activities in Europe*, https://www.oecd.org/cfe/leed/Social%20entrepreneurship%20policy%20brief%20EN_FINAL.pdf.

OECD (2010), *Measuring Entrepreneurship: The OECD-Eurostat Entrepreneurship Indicators Programme*, OECD Statistics Brief, www.oecd.org/std/statisticsbrief.

OECD/EU (2015), *The Missing Entrepreneurs 2015: Policies for Self-employment and Entrepreneurship*, OECD Publishing, Paris, http://dx.doi.org/10.1787/9789264226418-en.

United Nations Department of Economic and Social Affairs (2010), *World Programme of Action for Youth: Action for Youth*, UN DESA, New York.

Youth Business International (2012), *Youth Entrepreneurship: A Contexts Framework*, YBI, London.

Youth Business International (2013), *Generation entrepreneur? The state of global youth entrepreneurship*, YBI, London.

Chapter 2

Portraits of youth entrepreneurs

Informal and subsistence self-employed activities are the dominant form of youth entrepreneurship in developing countries. Yet only a tiny portion of youth entrepreneurs record high performance levels in terms of profits and employment generation. This chapter provides a detailed portrait of youth entrepreneurs in Côte d'Ivoire, Madagascar, Peru and Viet Nam. It shows that young entrepreneurs are numerous and are less educated than young employees. They generally enter entrepreneurship for lack of other choices, and fare worse in terms of working conditions.

Youth accounted for one-sixth of the world's population in 2015 – 1.2 billion individuals – and their number is expected to increase by 7% by 2030 (UN DESA, 2015). Most live in the developing world, primarily in Asia and Africa. The youth population has reached its peak in all regions of the world except Africa, where it is expected to double to more than 830 million by 2050. While the youth bulge constitutes a real opportunity for achieving a demographic dividend, it also poses a complex employment challenge. Absorbing the youth bulge is a challenge for developing countries, especially in Africa and South Asia (OECD, 2015). Incomplete or not yet started demographic transition in low-income countries, in particular in the African continent, as reflected by the explosion in young people, will become a source of major stresses if they cannot be provided with enough jobs (OECD, 2015; AfDB/OECD/UNDP, 2015). As many as 600 million jobs will need to be created worldwide over the next 15 years to keep employment rates at their current level (World Bank, 2012). In Africa, almost 30 million additional jobs will need to be created every year (AfDB/OECD/UNDP, 2015). In this continent, youth employment is largely a problem of quality in low-income countries (vulnerable employment and working poverty) and one of quantity in middle-income countries (unemployment, discouragement or inactivity). More young people are discouraged than unemployed in Africa, suggesting that the youth employment challenge has been underestimated (AfDB et al., 2012).

In developing countries, creating more and better jobs is one of the major challenges. Formal labour markets are far from able to absorb the continuous flow of young entrants. Wage employment opportunities are scarce and formal job creation insufficient to give most youth a chance to access decent work. In contexts where poverty is widespread and social safety nets like unemployment benefits are almost non-existent, most individuals cannot afford to remain unemployed and have no choice but to take whatever job they find. This situation often results in individuals, and in particular young people, ending up engaging in self-employed informal and subsistence activities.

Many young people engage in entrepreneurship

The countries studied in this report illustrate the diversity of the developing world. Youth entrepreneurs from Côte d'Ivoire, Madagascar, Peru and Viet Nam operate in rather different conditions that reflect the developing world's diversity, in terms of both geographical location and income level. The four countries exhibit highly unequal income levels and are at different stages of development. Madagascar, classified as a low-income economy, is the poorest country of the sample, with a gross national income (GNI) per capita of USD 450. Côte d'Ivoire and Viet Nam are lower-middle-income economies, although Viet Nam shows a markedly higher income level. Peru stands out as an upper-middle-income economy with a GNI per capita 14 times greater than that of Madagascar, 4 times greater than that of Côte d'Ivoire and 3 times greater than that of Viet Nam. Côte d'Ivoire and Viet Nam are recording the fastest economic growth, however. There are also important differences across the four countries in terms of population size, human development outcomes and other economic indicators (Table 2.1).

Youth entrepreneurship is a significant phenomenon. It is defined as comprising all non-farm household unincorporated businesses operated by youth, either as own-account workers or employers. Its relative extent varies greatly across countries, ranging from 14% in Viet Nam to 43.9% in Côte d'Ivoire, where the percentage represents the total employed youth population outside agriculture as the main occupation (Figure 2.1). Entrepreneurship is more common in poorer countries (Côte d'Ivoire, Madagascar) where wage employment opportunities are less abundant, suggesting a negative correlation with the level of development. If agriculture had been included, entrepreneurship would have reached higher levels, since the majority of agricultural production units are unincorporated operating on a small scale at the household level with scarce presence of employees. For the reasons explained in the previous chapter, agriculture is not taken into account in this report and is excluded from the empirical analysis.

Table 2.1. **Selected demographic, social and economic indicators by country, 2014**

	Côte d'Ivoire	Madagascar	Peru	Viet Nam
GNI per capita, Atlas method (current USD)	1 450	450	6 370	1 900
GDP growth (annual %)	8.5	3.1	2.4	6.0
Inflation, GDP deflator (annual %)	0.9	10.1	3.0	3.7
Total population (thousands), 2015	22 157	23 571	30 973	90 728
Youth population 15-29 (thousands), 2015	6 315	6 854	8 298	24 440
Fertility rate, total (births per woman)	5.0	4.4	2.5	2.0
Life expectancy at birth, total (years)	51.6	65.1	74.5	75.6
Net enrolment rate, primary (%)*	74.7	-	92.8	98.0
Net enrolment rate, secondary (%)**	-	31.1	78.4	-
Gross enrolment ratio, tertiary (%)***	8.7	4.2	40.5	30.5
Agriculture, value added (% of GDP)	22.4	25.1	7.2	17.7
Industry, value added (% of GDP)	21.1	17.2	35.2	33.2
Manufacturing, value added (% of GDP)	12.6	-	15.3	13.2
Services, value added (% of GDP)	56.5	57.7	57.6	39.0
Time required to start a business (days)	7	12	26	34
Internet users (per 100 people)	14.6	3.7	40.2	48.3

Note: * Not available in Madagascar all years and in Peru for 2013. ** Not available in Côte d'Ivoire. *** 2013 data for Madagascar and 2010 data for Peru.
Source: UN DESA World Population Prospects: The 2015 Revision, (https://esa.un.org/unpd/wpp/Download/Standard/Population/; accessed: December 2016), and World Bank Development Indicators (http://data.worldbank.org/data-catalog/world-development-indicators; accessed: December 2016)

Figure 2.1. **Distribution of workers by employment status, main occupation**

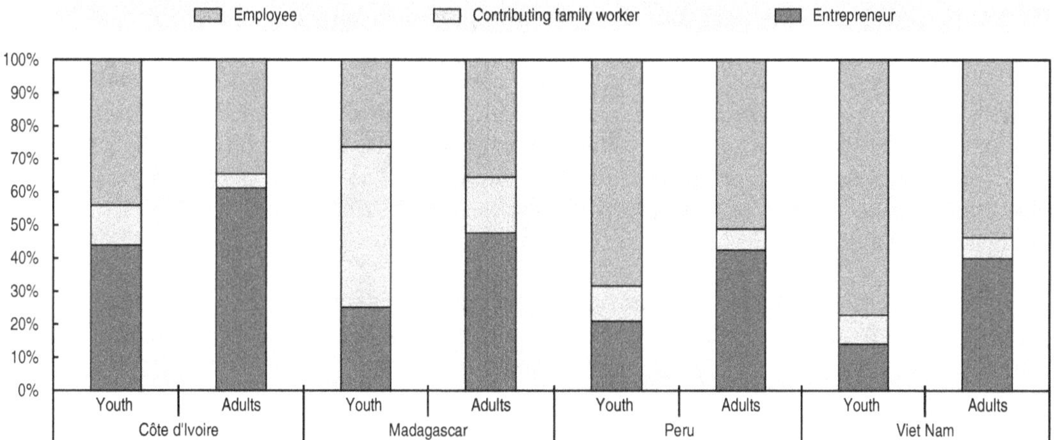

Note: Agriculture excluded. Entrepreneurs comprise own-account workers and employers. Youth are aged 15-29 and adults 30-64.
Source: Côte d'Ivoire ENSETE 2014, Madagascar ENEMPSI 2012, Peru ENAHO 2014, and Viet Nam LFS 2014.

As countries develop economically, more youth can be found in wage employment. Youth are far less engaged in entrepreneurship than adults, and work substantially more as employees, especially in richer countries (Viet Nam, Peru). This finding can be explained to some extent by a life-cycle effect: the inherent characteristics of youth, starting with their younger age and consequently lower work experience, result in segmented labour markets across ages. This pattern does not hold in poorer countries. In Madagascar, for instance, youth are less involved than adults in both entrepreneurship and wage employment, and are disproportionately concentrated in contributing family work. Although youth systematically outnumber adults in contributing family work across developing countries, their proportion declines dramatically as economies reach higher levels of income.

The vast majority of entrepreneurs are own-account workers. This is particularly true of youth. The number of youth employers is very small and does not exceed 1.5% of total youth employment (Figure 2.2). By contrast, adults work as employers two to five times more frequently. However, their number barely reaches 5.7% at most in the case of Peru. In other words, there are signs that most entrepreneurs, youth to a larger extent than adults, have not been able to generate jobs through their businesses.

Figure 2.2. Shares of own-account workers and employers, main occupation

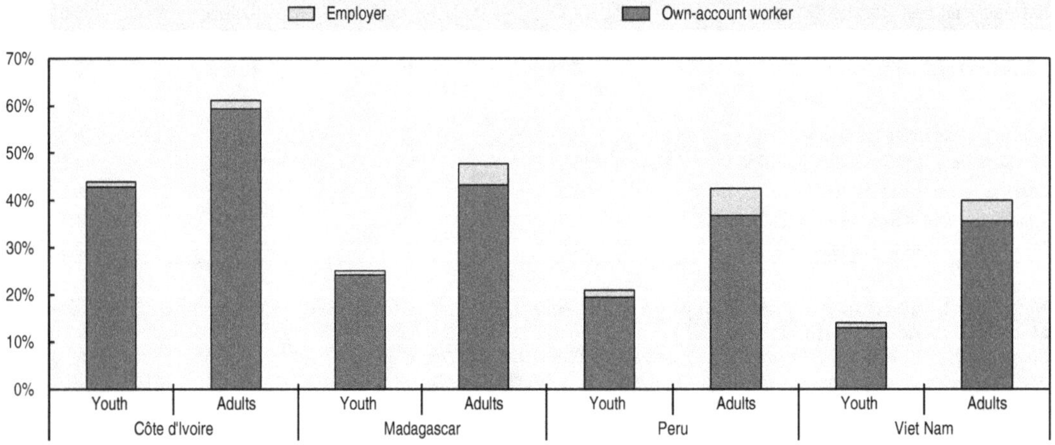

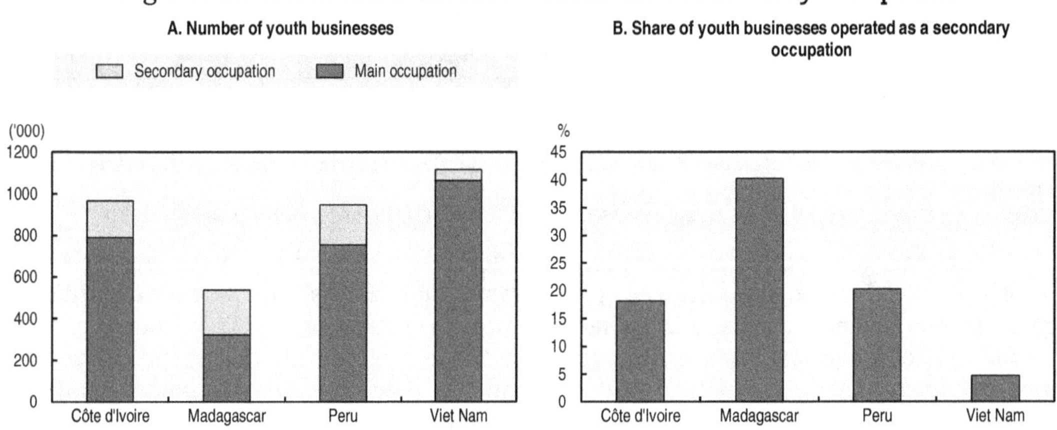

Note: Agriculture excluded. Youth are aged 15-29 and adults 30-64.
Source: Côte d'Ivoire ENSETE 2014, Madagascar ENEMPSI 2012, Peru ENAHO 2014, and Viet Nam LFS 2014.

Youth-run businesses account for a non-negligible share of all businesses. Youth businesses number nearly 1.1 million in Viet Nam, 1 million in Peru and Côte d'Ivoire, and 540 000 in Madagascar (Figure 2.3A). However, they account for a relatively small share of the total number of businesses, especially in more advanced economies: 11.2% in Viet Nam, 17.4% in Peru, 27.2% in Madagascar and 29.1% in Côte d'Ivoire. Some youth businesses are operated as a secondary occupation. The share of youth businesses operated as a secondary occupation ranges from 5% in Viet Nam to as high as 40% in Madagascar (Figure 2.3B).

Figure 2.3. Youth-run businesses as main or secondary occupation

Note: Agriculture excluded. Youth are aged 15-29.
Source: Côte d'Ivoire ENSETE 2014, Madagascar ENEMPSI 2012, Peru ENAHO 2014, and Viet Nam LFS 2014.

Multiple job-holding is more prevalent in lower-income economies, where the main occupation, whether wage labour or self-employment, often does not suffice to make a living. This pushes workers to engage in additional productive activities such as own-account work to improve their financial situation. In fact, 19% of young workers in Madagascar run a business in addition to their main job, three times more than in richer countries (Côte d'Ivoire, Viet Nam and Peru) (Figure 2.4). This situation primarily affects youth with a main job in agriculture, reflecting the importance of seasonality in agricultural production and the subsequent need to mitigate risks by diversifying income sources through off-farm side businesses.

Figure 2.4. **Share of young workers running a business in addition to their main occupation**

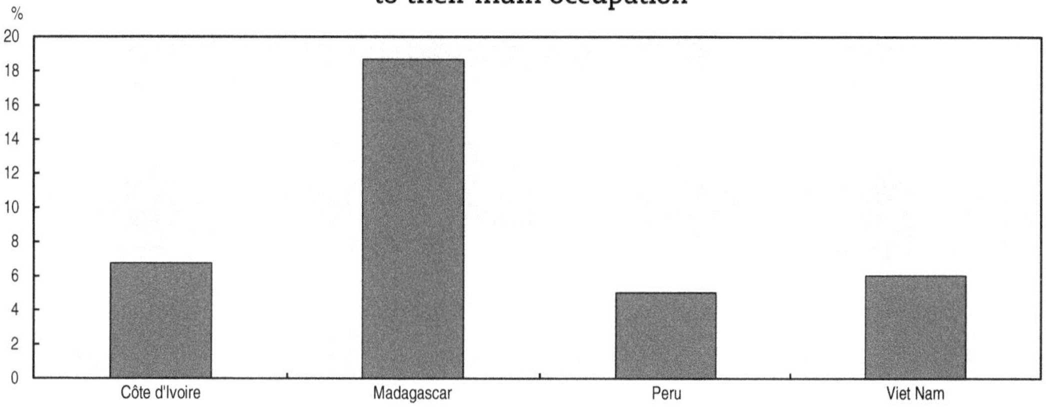

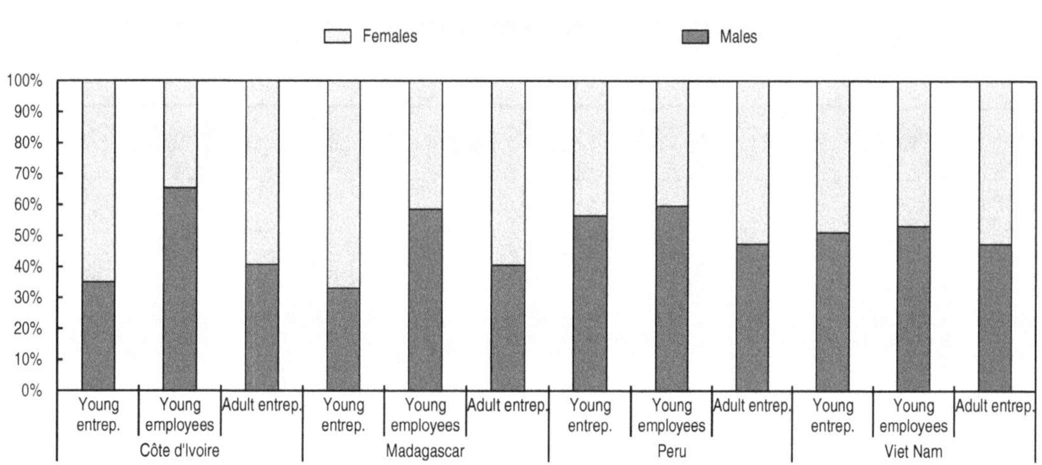

Note: Agriculture excluded. Youth are aged 15-29.
Source: Côte d'Ivoire ENSETE 2014, Madagascar ENEMPSI 2012, Peru ENAHO 2014, and Viet Nam LFS 2014.

Poorly educated and rural non-farm entrepreneurs predominate

There seems to be a tendency for women to be entrepreneurs in poorer countries. In Côte d'Ivoire and Madagascar, young entrepreneurs are predominantly female and young employees mostly male, whereas in Peru and Viet Nam males account for the majority of both young entrepreneurs and employees (Figure 2.5). Within youth entrepreneurship, the employers' segment is overwhelmingly male-dominated. In all countries, especially in less advanced ones (Côte d'Ivoire and Madagascar), adult entrepreneurship is primarily composed of women. The empirical literature has extensively documented women's labour market disadvantages in developing countries, in particular the specific barriers to decent wage employment and disproportionate concentration in less rewarding but more accessible self-employed work, often as supplemental activities for household survival (e.g. Arbache et al., 2010).

Figure 2.5. **Distribution of workers by main occupation and gender**

Note: Agriculture excluded. Youth are aged 15-29 and adults 30-64.
Source: Côte d'Ivoire ENSETE 2014, Madagascar ENEMPSI 2012, Peru ENAHO 2014, and Viet Nam LFS 2014.

Youth from rural areas are more likely to be entrepreneurs than their urban counterparts. This holds true even when agriculture is not included. For both adults and youth, entrepreneurship is more pronounced in rural areas (Figure 2.6). This reflects the fact that the countries under study are still predominantly rural. However, entrepreneurs from urban areas are more frequently employers and less often own-account workers than those from rural areas, highlighting the higher potential of urban entrepreneurship in terms of job creation.

Figure 2.6. **Share of young and adult entrepreneurs among workers by area of residence**

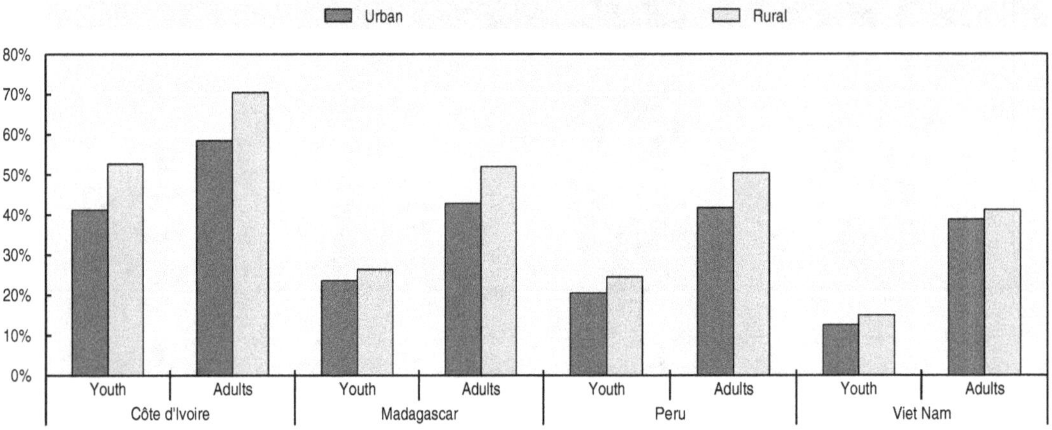

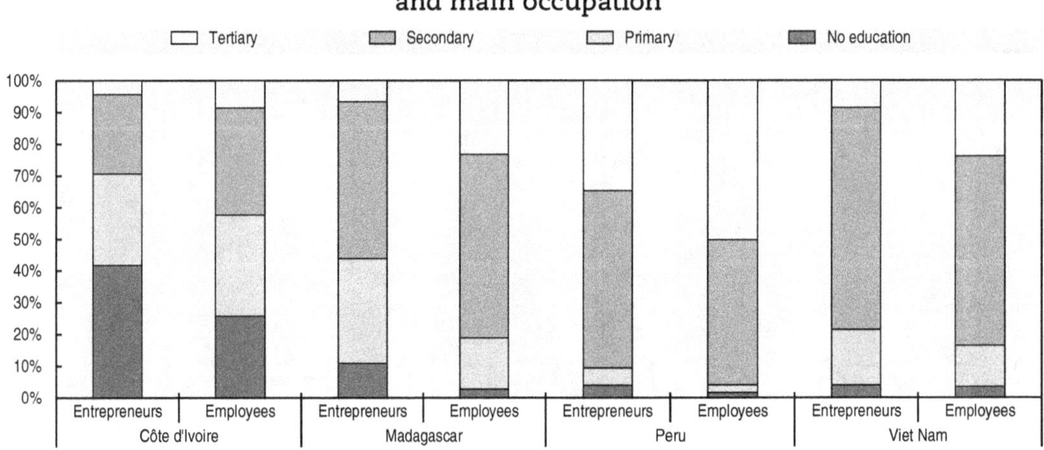

Note: Agriculture excluded. Youth are aged 15-29 and adults 30-64.
Source: Côte d'Ivoire ENSETE 2014, Madagascar ENEMPSI 2012, Peru ENAHO 2014, and Viet Nam LFS 2014.

A minority of youth entrepreneurs are highly educated. This holds true especially in the less advanced countries. Youth with no educational background or with only a primary level abound in entrepreneurship in Madagascar and Côte d'Ivoire, representing 43.9% and 70.7%, respectively (Figure 2.7). In sharp contrast, they represent only 21.4% of young entrepreneurs in Viet Nam and 9.4% in Peru. Wage-employed youth are better educated, especially in wealthier countries. At the same time, it is worth noting that a small portion of youth entrepreneurship is made up of highly educated workers, for example 4.3% in Côte d'Ivoire and 8.5% in Viet Nam. Peru is far ahead, with the share of young entrepreneurs with a tertiary education rising to 34.7%. Hence there exists a niche of young entrepreneurs whose education has equipped them to run successful businesses, and this niche group appears to grow with economic development.

Figure 2.7. **Distribution of young workers by level of education and main occupation**

Note: Agriculture excluded. Youth are aged 15-29.
Source: Côte d'Ivoire ENSETE 2014, Madagascar ENEMPSI 2012, Peru ENAHO 2014, and Viet Nam LFS 2014.

Ethnic minorities are disproportionately concentrated among entrepreneurs. Married young people also turn to entrepreneurship more often than to wage employment. Ethnic minorities around the world face deprivation of many sorts, from income poverty to limited access to basic infrastructure and services, not to mention low educational attainment, health issues, poor earnings and, ultimately, discrimination (Hall and Patrinos, 2012). Often, for ethnic minorities, engaging in entrepreneurship is a way to cope with and escape extreme poverty. In Côte d'Ivoire and Viet Nam, youth account for more ethnic minority entrepreneurs than the older generation (Table 2.2). Turning to marital status and family composition, youth running a business are more often married than are young employees, and married youth generally live with more dependents within the household than young employees do.

Table 2.2. **Selected workers' characteristics**

		Côte d'Ivoire	Madagascar	Peru	Viet Nam
Age	Young entrepreneurs	24.6	23.7	23.8	25.4
	Young employees	23.2	23.5	23.4	24.2
	Adult entrepreneurs	41.8	43.5	47.0	45.8
Ethnic minorities (%)	Young entrepreneurs	23.2	-	15.1	6.5
	Young employees	14.0	-	14.1	7.8
	Adult entrepreneurs	21.5	-	17.4	5.0
Married (%)	Young entrepreneurs	52.9	65.4	39.2	64.2
	Young employees	19.4	43.9	21.0	43.2
	Adult entrepreneurs	69.3	75.0	70.3	86.8
Household size	Young entrepreneurs	4.7	3.7	5.0	4.5
	Young employees	4.9	3.9	5.0	4.3
	Adult entrepreneurs	5.3	4.5	4.4	3.9
Household dependency ratio (%)	Young entrepreneurs	41.3	14.9	37.1	32.2
	Young employees	37.1	19.0	35.3	26.0
	Adult entrepreneurs	47.6	23.2	38.9	36.2

Note: Agriculture excluded. Youth are aged 15-29 and adults 30-64. Household dependency ratio is the percentage share of non-working members within the household.
Source: Côte d'Ivoire ENSETE 2014, Madagascar ENEMPSI 2012, Peru ENAHO 2014, and Viet Nam LFS 2014.

Young people often appear to go into business for lack of a better job

A large majority of youth entrepreneurs say they are running a business by choice. Yet many youth appear to enter entrepreneurship due to the lack of decent job opportunities. A total of 56% of youth entrepreneurs in Madagascar and 71% in Viet Nam declare that they are running a business by choice (Figure 2.8). Young people in these countries say they entered entrepreneurship with a desire to become independent or to obtain a higher income, among other reasons. By contrast, youth entrepreneurship in Peru is primarily motivated by necessity, due, for instance, to the lack of wage employment opportunities (52%). Necessity-driven entrepreneurship dominates in urban areas and choice-driven in rural areas in poorer countries (Madagascar and Viet Nam), while the reverse is true in richer countries (Peru). This suggests that choice-driven youth entrepreneurs tend to move from rural to urban areas with economic development. The share of youth businesses operated by family tradition is relatively small, reaching at most 19% in the case of Viet Nam. Accordingly, family business transfers from one generation to the next or the influence of the parents' occupation are rather marginal drivers of youth entrepreneurship. Compared to youth, adults in entrepreneurship appear to be more necessity driven in richer countries (Peru and Viet Nam), but not in poorer ones (Madagascar). This could be indicative of a generational transition towards higher quality entrepreneurship with economic development.

Figure 2.8. **Distribution of young entrepreneurs by motivation for running a business**

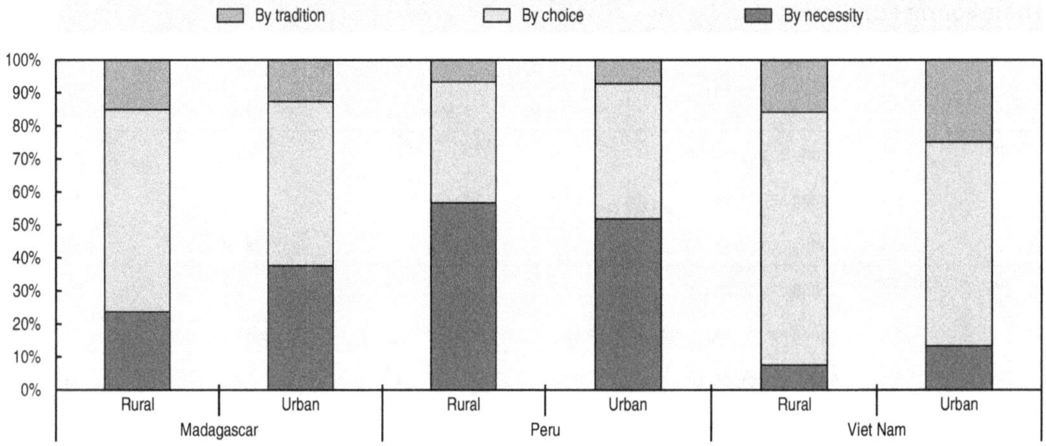

Note: Agriculture excluded. Youth are aged 15-29.
Source: Madagascar ENEMPSI 2012, Peru ENAHO 2014, and Viet Nam HBIS 2014.

Underemployment and multiple job holding are prevalent among youth entrepreneurs. As these phenomena occur less often among youth employees, it suggests that the decision to enter entrepreneurship is most likely driven by necessity. Job satisfaction, measured as the percentage of workers who declare being very satisfied with their main occupation, is not markedly different between youth entrepreneurs and the wage employed. Yet youth entrepreneurs are more likely than youth employees to be looking for another job, wishing to work more hours (time-related underemployment) or holding multiple jobs (Table 2.3). These findings suggest that entrepreneurship is to a large extent necessity driven and composed of subsistence activities. Moreover, they reflect the fact the youth employment challenge in developing countries is to a large extent driven by poor aggregate demand. For instance, in Africa, country experts consider insufficient labour demand as the biggest obstacles to youth in the labour market, and young people themselves agree that a lack of jobs is the most pressing issue (AfDB et al., 2012). To tackle the challenges young people face in African labour markets, policy makers must address bottlenecks constraining the demand for labour, while at the same time helping young people to obtain the skills to succeed in a tough labour market. Accordingly, the lack of wage employment opportunities for youth, which forces many of them to enter entrepreneurship, is probably a leading cause of youth business failure in developing settings.

Young entrepreneurs are nonetheless optimistic about the future. It is interesting to note that the vast majority of young entrepreneurs, 66.6% in Madagascar and 77.6% in Viet Nam, see a future for their business (Figure 2.9) (data not available in Côte d'Ivoire and Peru). Young entrepreneurs are also more optimistic in rural areas and, in the case of Viet Nam, as compared to adults. What is also remarkable is that a substantial proportion of young entrepreneurs, in Madagascar more than in Viet Nam, want their children to take over their business, especially among rural dwellers. Their number is, however, not as high as that of adult entrepreneurs in Madagascar. It is worth noting that these positive perceptions of youth about their business in Madagascar and Viet Nam are significantly higher in manufacturing than in trade and especially services, which are typically considered, in the context of developing countries, as free-entry sectors in that they generally require low levels of capital and skills.

Table 2.3. **Selected indicators on job quality**

	Viet Nam		Madagascar		Côte d'Ivoire		Peru	
	Rural	**Urban**	**Rural**	**Urban**	**Rural**	**Urban**	**Rural**	**Urban**
Job satisfaction (%)								
Young entrepreneurs	-	-	19.5	21.1	17.9	15.2	-	-
Young employees	-	-	11.7	13.0	16.3	19.3	-	-
Adult entrepreneurs	-	-	22.7	19.7	21.3	15.4	-	-
Looking for another job (%)								
Young entrepreneurs	-	-	8.4	14.4	11.0	14.9	5.7	10.1
Young employees	-	-	6.3	8.6	12.5	17.6	4.9	7.9
Adult entrepreneurs	-	-	5.0	7.3	7.3	13.3	3.5	4.3
Time-related underemployment (%)								
Young entrepreneurs	7.1	4.2	18.7	22.2	31.1	33.8	11.8	12.4
Young employees	3.4	2.0	13.0	12.8	31.8	32.6	8.6	7.6
Adult entrepreneurs	4.2	2.5	12.5	14.1	20.5	28.1	8.7	9.0
Multiple job holding (%)								
Young entrepreneurs	23.8	4.7	37.3	27.4	15.3	5.6	23.2	10.7
Young employees	3.0	0.8	17.1	8.6	7.1	4.8	7.6	8.3
Adult entrepreneurs	29.5	7.5	46.9	32.8	14.7	7.8	26.7	15.8

Note: Agriculture excluded. Youth are aged 15-29 and adults 30-64. Job satisfaction refers to the percentage share of workers who declare being very satisfied with their main occupation. Time-related underemployment corresponds to the percentage share of workers who declare that they are willing and available to increase their working time with respect to their main job (Côte d'Ivoire, Madagascar) or to all jobs held (Peru and Viet Nam). *Source:* Côte d'Ivoire ENSETE 2014, Madagascar ENEMPSI 2012, Peru ENAHO 2014, and Viet Nam LFS 2014.

Figure 2.9. **Perceptions of youth and adult entrepreneurs on future of the business**

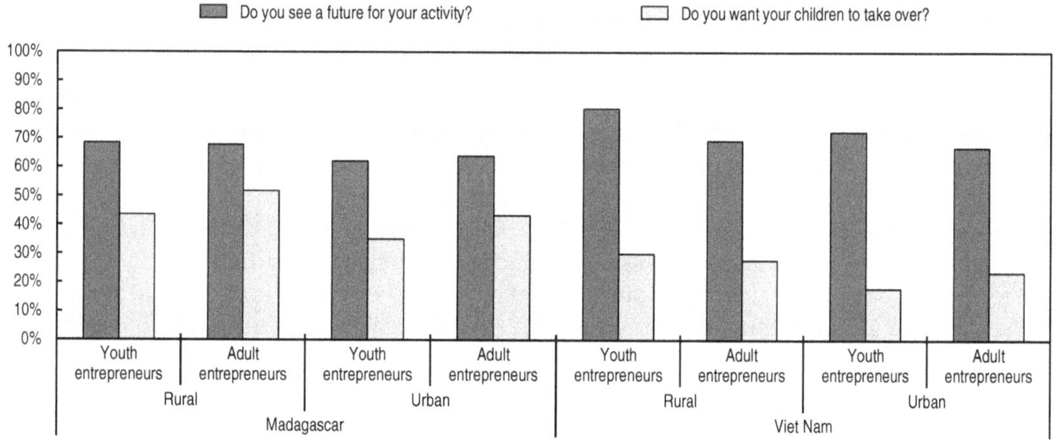

Note: Agriculture excluded. Youth are aged 15-29 and adults 30-64.
Source: Madagascar ENEMPSI 2012 and Viet Nam HBIS 2014.

Few youth entrepreneurs possess basic business skills

Young entrepreneurs appear to possess very limited business skills. Information on business skills shows that very few young entrepreneurs make use of written accounts, from 11% in Madagascar to 34% in Viet Nam (Figure 2.10). Bookkeeping is particularly infrequent in rural areas. Only in Viet Nam are young entrepreneurs more inclined than adults to keep written accounts. In Madagascar and Viet Nam, moreover, a large majority of young entrepreneurs do not adopt any business strategy at all, respectively 72% and 61% (no information available on business strategies for Côte d'Ivoire and Peru). Young entrepreneurs in Viet Nam are nonetheless much more likely than adults to adopt a business strategy, especially in rural areas. Rather than actual strategic thinking aiming at optimising market position, business strategy must be understood here as simple steps taken to prospect for new customers or to reduce costs by renewing suppliers, limiting manpower costs or moving to less costly premises. When young entrepreneurs develop a business strategy, it is most often limited to prospecting for new customers. In Viet Nam, young entrepreneurs are twice as likely as adults to adopt such a strategy in rural areas, and a non-negligible share of young entrepreneurs (22%) actively look for alternative suppliers to reduce costs. Other cost-reduction strategies, including optimising manpower and premises costs, are almost non-existent. In Madagascar, young entrepreneurs lack business strategies apart from active prospection of new customers, and this concerns a very limited number of them.

Figure 2.10. **Incidence of bookkeeping**

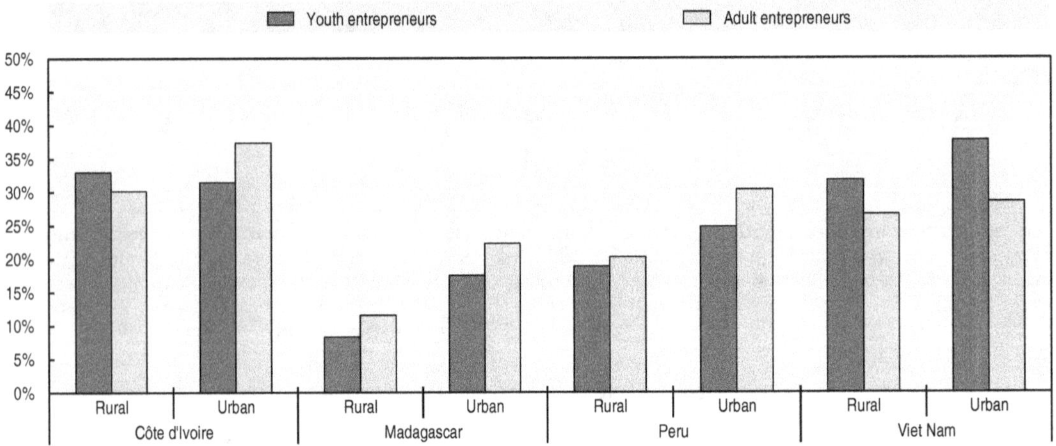

Note: Agriculture excluded. Youth are aged 15-29 and adults 30-64.
Source: Côte d'Ivoire ENSETE 2014, Madagascar ENEMPSI 2012, Peru ENAHO 2014, and Viet Nam HBIS 2014.

Very few young entrepreneurs display business acumen. Available data in Madagascar show first that almost none of them set prices in accordance with production costs. This is not surprising given that only a tiny minority of Malagasy young entrepreneurs actually keep written accounts (Figure 2.11). Second, barely one-fifth of them are willing to recruit workers outside the family nucleus. This can be problematic given that family members may not possess the necessary skills and competencies, thus hampering business performance and in particular labour productivity (Nguyen and Nordman, 2014). Third, no more than 13% of young entrepreneurs in Madagascar have a strategy to cope with economic shocks.

Figure 2.11. **Business practices in Madagascar**

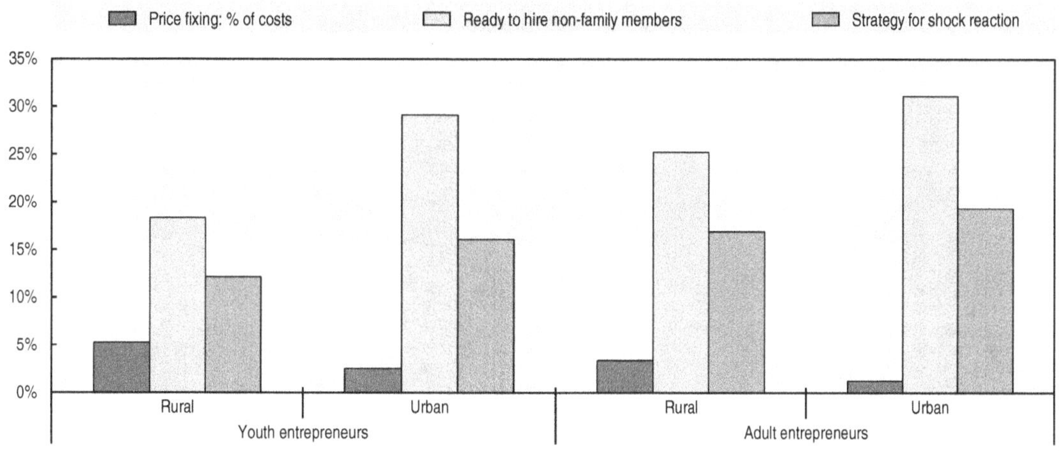

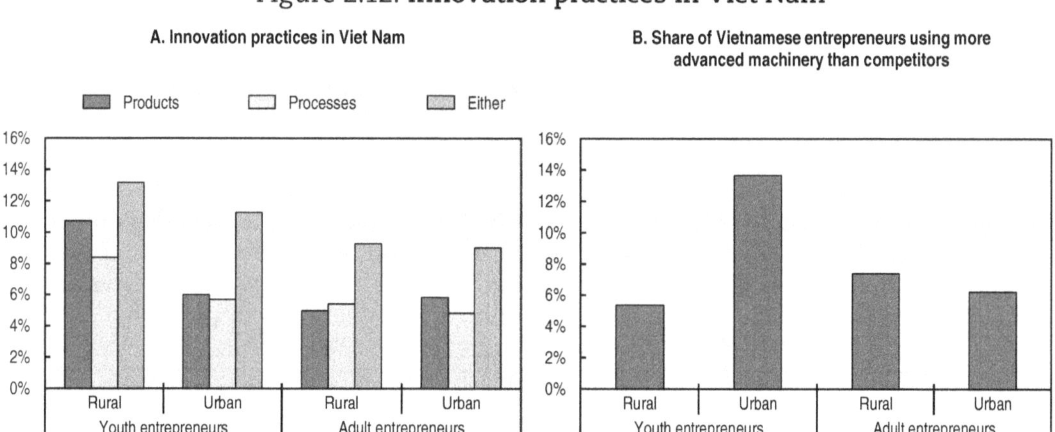

Note: Agriculture excluded. Youth are aged 15-29 and adults 30-64.
Source: Madagascar ENEMPSI 2012.

Innovation is limited and more frequent among youth entrepreneurs than adults in Viet Nam. A central element of managerial capital is innovation. This information is available in the Vietnamese data in two dimensions: offering new products or services, and introducing new production processes. A total of 12% of Vietnamese young entrepreneurs innovate by either means. This is a non-negligible share and surpasses the adult share, especially in rural areas. Innovation in terms of products or services is slightly more frequent among young entrepreneurs with respect to processes (Figure 2.12 A). In the same vein, a number of young entrepreneurs in Viet Nam also "innovate" in terms of equipment by using more advanced machinery than competitors, and their share exceeds that of adults in urban areas (Figure 2.12 B).

Figure 2.12. **Innovation practices in Viet Nam**

A. Innovation practices in Viet Nam

B. Share of Vietnamese entrepreneurs using more advanced machinery than competitors

Note: Agriculture excluded. Youth are aged 15-29 and adults 30-64.
Source: Viet Nam HBIS 2014.

Youth businesses are typically very small. They are also smaller than businesses owned by adults. Most young entrepreneurs work alone as own-account workers, from 53% in Viet Nam to 82% in Peru (Figure 2.13 A). Young entrepreneurs rarely have employees, and when they do, the average number is extremely low, reaching only about 1.5 employees across the surveyed countries. The notable exception is Côte d'Ivoire, where young employers have on average 2.2 employees (Figure 2.13 B). This result echoes recent empirical evidence showing that the average size of informal production units across the developing world stands at around 1.5 individuals (Cling et al., 2015).

Figure 2.13. **Characteristics of youth-run businesses compared to adult-run businesses**

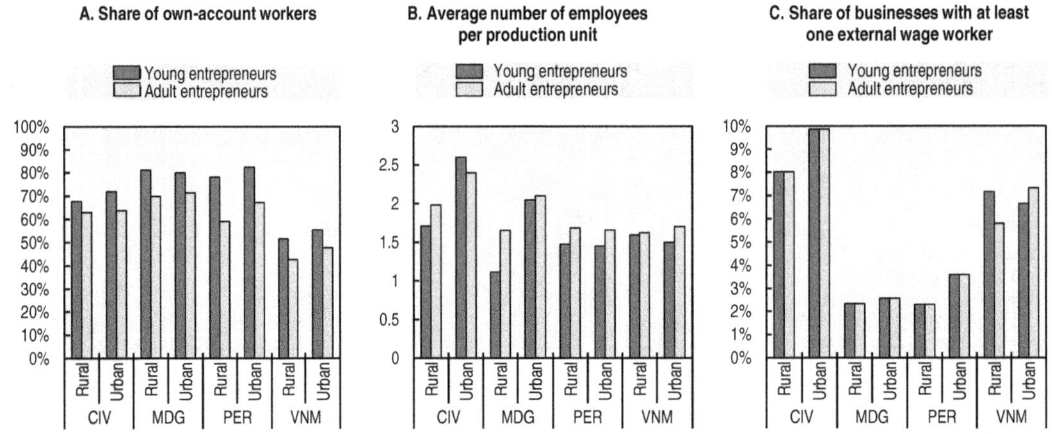

Note: Agriculture excluded. CIV refers to Côte d'Ivoire, MDG to Madagascar, PER to Peru and VNM to Viet Nam. Youth are aged 15-29 and adults 30-64.
Source: Côte d'Ivoire ENSETE 2014, Madagascar ENEMPSI 2012, Peru ENAHO 2014, and Viet Nam HBIS 2014.

Youth businesses primarily operate in services and trade. These are often referred to as free-entry sectors. In developing countries, services and trade often require low levels of capital and skills, and this facilitates entry into entrepreneurship. Youth entrepreneurship's sectorial allocation actually depends on the level of development. In Côte d'Ivoire and Madagascar, where entrepreneurship is to a large extent driven by necessity and associated with subsistence activities, youth businesses are far more often engaged in trade and less in services, while the reverse is true in Peru and Viet Nam (Figures 2.14 A and 2.14 B). Manufacturing is quite uncommon for youth businesses in the four countries, especially in Peru and Côte d'Ivoire. Evidence from advanced economies shows that young entrepreneurs tend to privilege services over other sectors, in particular manufacturing (OECD, 2013). In industrialised countries, this is partly due to the deindustrialisation process. In developing countries, however, it results instead from an underdeveloped manufacturing sector with significant entry barriers that disproportionately affect youth. Starting a business in the manufacturing sector generally requires higher levels of capital and investment, as well as more specific and advanced skills, than in other sectors (Shane, 2008; Parker, 2009). The limited presence of young entrepreneurs in manufacturing in developing countries can be also related to the poor working conditions usually offered by this sector, as evidenced by a number of studies (e.g. Blattman and Dercon, 2016). As regards Africa, the manufacturing sector is currently relatively small but new opportunities are emerging, in particular thanks to the possibilities offered by new technologies (AfDB/OECD/UNDP, 2017). Africa's entrepreneurial potential for industrialisation is high but untapped: entrepreneurs' contribution to industrialisation has been limited so far. Africa needs to leverage its pool of opportunity-driven entrepreneurs for industrialisation and help survival entrepreneurs to transition into the labour market.

A generational transition in sectorial allocation is also at stake. Youth businesses are more services oriented than adult businesses overall, and less often found in manufacturing and trade. Viet Nam stands apart, however, with youth businesses more present than adult businesses in manufacturing. This suggests that access barriers to this sector are not more binding for youth than for adults. In contrast with services, manufacturing is more prevalent in rural areas, especially in Peru, reflecting the importance of the agro-processing industries.

Figure 2.14. **Youth and adult businesses by sector of activity**

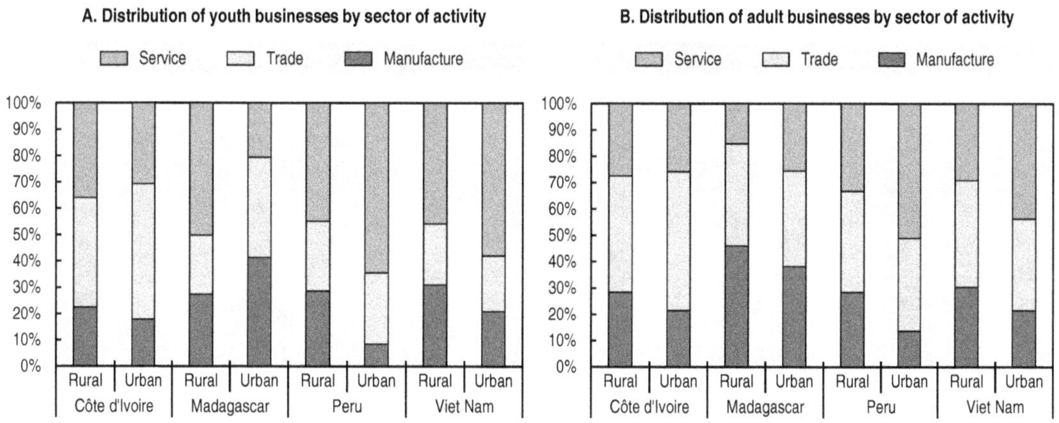

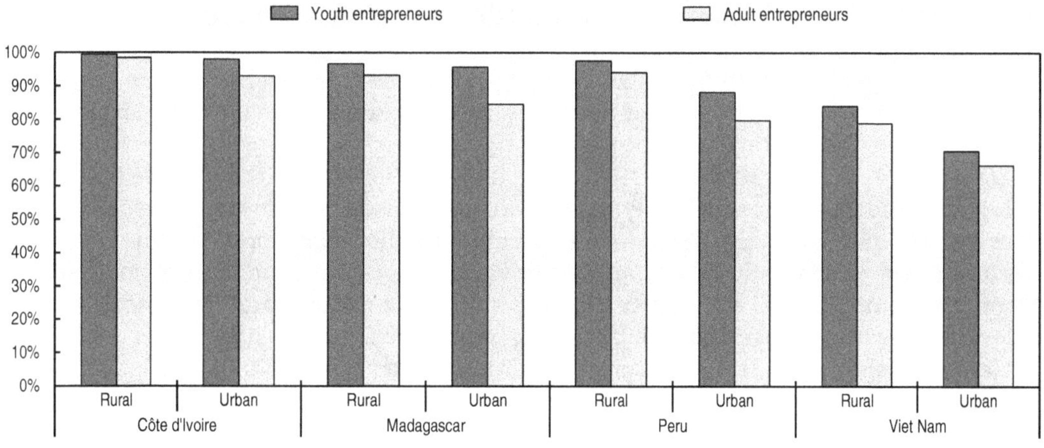

Note: Agriculture excluded. Youth are aged 15-29 and adults 30-64.
Source: Côte d'Ivoire ENSETE 2014, Madagascar ENEMPSI 2012, Peru ENAHO 2014, and Viet Nam HBIS 2014.

Informality is the norm. Almost all businesses in Cote d'Ivoire, Madagascar, Peru and Viet Nam are unregistered with the authorities. The extent of unregistered youth businesses is massive, ranging from 80% in Viet Nam to 98% in Côte d'Ivoire (Figure 2.15). Informality is more prevalent in rural areas, and it concerns youth businesses to a larger extent than adult businesses. Given the age difference, enterprises operated by youth are likely to have been created more recently, suggesting that informality could be more common at early stages of the business life cycle.

Figure 2.15. **Share of unregistered businesses**

Note: Agriculture excluded. Youth are aged 15-29 and adults 30-64.
Source: Côte d'Ivoire ENSETE 2014, Madagascar ENEMPSI 2012, Peru ENAHO 2014, and Viet Nam HBIS 2014.

Informality appears to be mostly the result of misinformation. A large number of youth running informal businesses in Peru (53%), Viet Nam (70%) and Madagascar (75%) believe that registration is simply not compulsory (Figure 2.16) (data not available for Côte d'Ivoire). This belief is particularly widespread in rural areas. In this respect, improving access to information on the regulatory framework and the benefits of formalisation will be an important element of a formalisation strategy.

Figure 2.16. **Distribution of youth unregistered businesses, by reason for not registering**

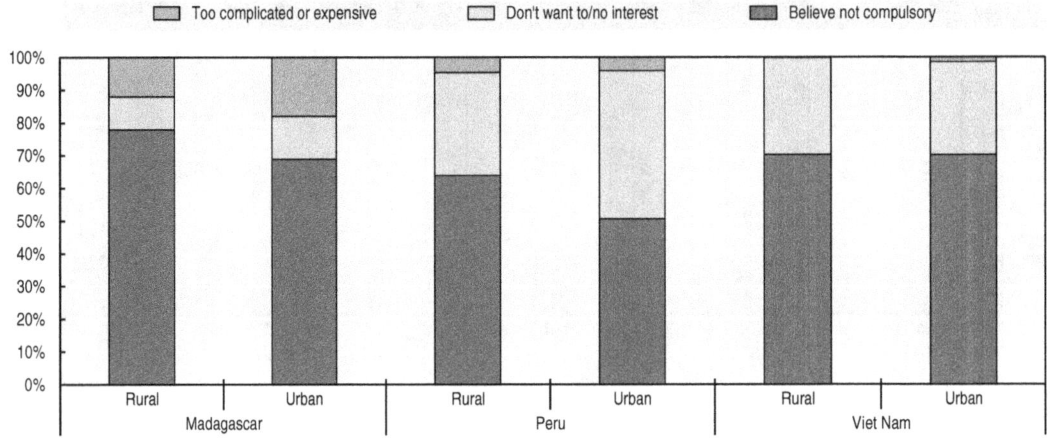

Note: Agriculture excluded. Youth are aged 15-29 and adults 30-64.
Source: Madagascar ENEMPSI 2012, Peru ENAHO 2014, and Viet Nam HBIS 2014.

Youth entrepreneurship is less financially rewarding than wage employment

The profits generated by young entrepreneurs are most often modest. They are below the level of income earned by youth in wage employment (Figure 2.17 A). On average in the four countries covered in this study, 96.2% of youth businesses recorded positive profits, but this aggregate estimate masks uneven patterns across countries depending on their level of development (Figure 2.17 B). In Peru and Viet Nam, the richest countries of the sample, almost no young entrepreneurs register negative or zero profits, while in Madagascar and Côte d'Ivoire, which are much less economically advanced, respectively 12% and 15% register negative or zero profits. Likewise, the level of profits generated by youth businesses appears to be positively associated with a country's development stage. In 2014, the average annual profits of youth businesses in Peru reached nearly USD 4 800 PPP, or 38%, 242% and 359% more than in Viet Nam, Côte d'Ivoire (data from 2012) and Madagascar, respectively (profits are annualised, adjusted for seasonality and converted to USD PPP to allow cross-country comparability). Entrepreneurship, especially in rural areas, is generally less financially rewarding for youth than wage employment. More than four out of five young entrepreneurs in Côte d'Ivoire and Peru record profits below the average wage earned by young employees. In the two other countries, entrepreneurship appears to be more economically attractive: 38% of youth businesses in Madagascar and 43% in Viet Nam report profits that do not fall below the average wage of young employees.

Figure 2.17. **Profits of youth businesses**

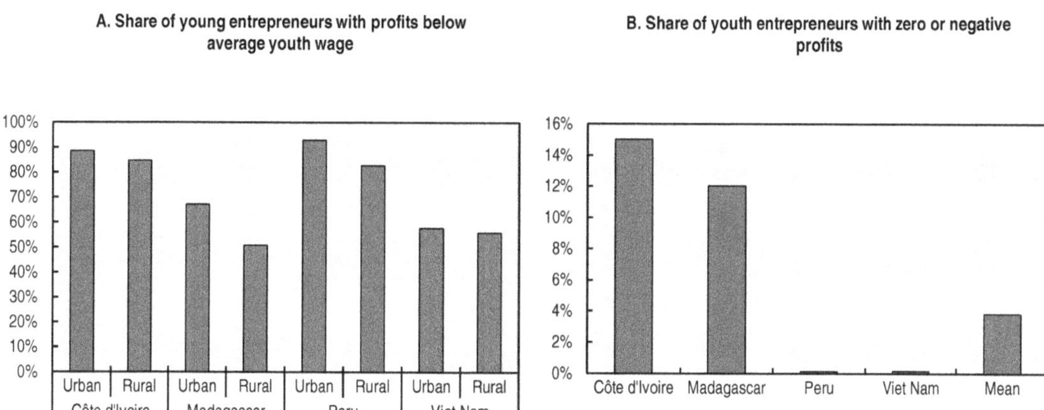

Note: Agriculture excluded. Youth are aged 15-29 and adults 30-64.
Source: Côte d'Ivoire ENSETE 2014, Madagascar ENEMPSI 2012, Peru ENAHO 2014, and Viet Nam HBIS 2014.

The distribution of profits is more unequal in the more advanced countries. Figure 2.18 displays the quintile distribution of youth businesses' average annual profits by country. In line with previous findings, youth businesses at the upper end of the distribution, in particular those in the top quintile, generate far greater profits in Viet Nam, and above all in Peru, than those in the lower quintiles, while in Côte d'Ivoire, and especially in Madagascar, the distribution is much less unequal. In other words, in more economically advanced countries, such as Viet Nam and Peru, the profit-generating capacity of top earners is much higher than those at the lower end of the distribution.

Figure 2.18. **Quintile distribution of youth businesses' average annual profits, in USD PPP**

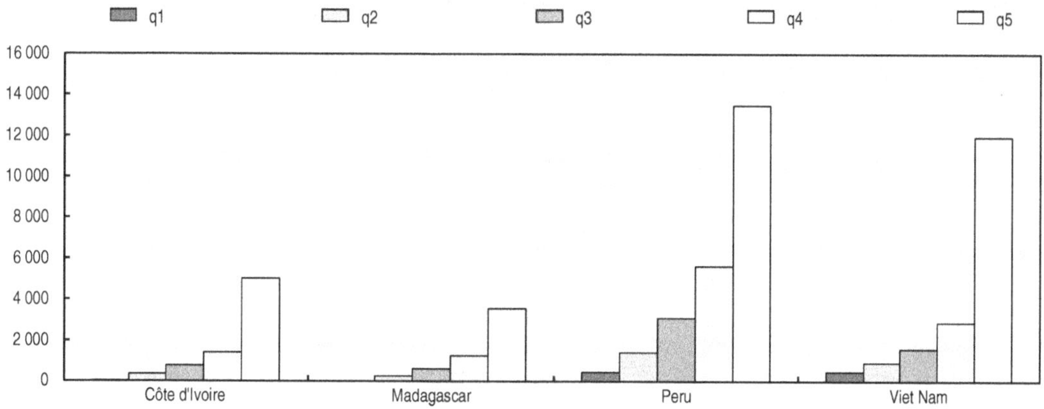

Note: Agriculture excluded. Youth are aged 15-29.
Source: Côte d'Ivoire ENSETE 2014, Madagascar ENEMPSI 2012, Peru ENAHO 2014, and Viet Nam HBIS 2014.

Relatively few youth businesses generate employment. About 21% of youth businesses surveyed in Côte d'Ivoire and Viet Nam had grown in size since their inception (Figure 2.19 A). In Madagascar, this share falls to 5% (data not available for Peru). The average employment growth rate of youth businesses since their inception stands at 5% in Madagascar, 19% in Viet Nam, and 30% in Côte d'Ivoire (Figure 2.19 B). However, as the vast majority of youth business owners started alone – more than two-thirds in Viet Nam and four-fifths in Côte d'Ivoire and Madagascar – the number of jobs created is in fact very limited. Indeed, most youth businesses that generated employment had only recruited one worker since business inception. This is the case for 68% of such businesses in Côte d'Ivoire, 80% in Viet Nam and 88% in Madagascar.

Youth entrepreneurs recruit mainly family members. The propensity of youth business owners to recruit outside the family nucleus is extremely low (Figure 2.13 C). In Madagascar, only 2% have offered a job to at least one external wage worker. The other countries do not do much better in this respect. Overall, the employment generation capacity of youth businesses, especially in Madagascar, is marginal. Youth businesses typically start very small and tend to remain so. By contrast, adult entrepreneurs are more often employers than young entrepreneurs, and they generally account for more employees and recruit more outside the family sphere.

Figure 2.19. **Growth of youth businesses**

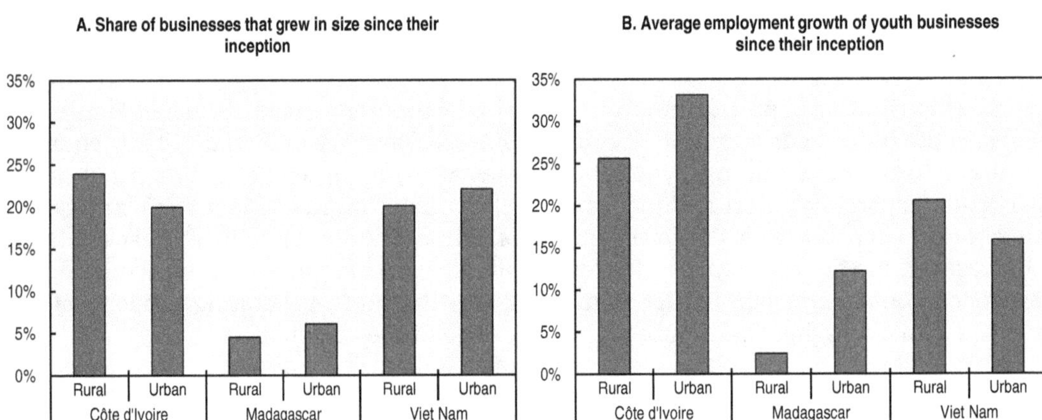

Note: Agriculture excluded. Youth are aged 15-29.
Source: Côte d'Ivoire ENSETE 2014, Madagascar ENEMPSI 2012, and Viet Nam HBIS 2014.

A tiny proportion of youth entrepreneurs can be considered top performers. Based on the criteria of profitability and job creation, youth businesses can be classified into three performance segments: i) top performers; ii) mid performers; and iii) low performers. Top performers include youth businesses that recorded the highest profits (top tertile of the distribution of profits) and also generated employment since their inception (for Peru, the job creation criterion is replaced by the presence of external wage workers since information on initial employment size is missing). Mid performers comprise those youth businesses with the highest profits (top tertile) that did not create jobs and youth businesses with intermediate levels of profits (second tertile). Finally, low performers refer to youth businesses with the lowest profits (bottom tertile). This categorisation, which combines two major outcomes of entrepreneurial performance, allows the classification of youth businesses into three steps of the entrepreneurial performance ladder. The share of youth businesses that combine the highest profits with job creation is, not surprisingly, very low, reaching at most 8.4% in the case of Côte d'Ivoire (Figure 2.20). Madagascar lags far behind, with only 1.7% of youth businesses classified as top performers. It is worth mentioning that, among the highest profit earners, job creation is strongly associated with increased profit-generating capacity, especially in Peru and even more so in Viet Nam. In Viet Nam, top performers record average profits 116% greater than those of the highest profits earners that did not create jobs. In Peru, the figure is 63%, while in Côte d'Ivoire and Madagascar, the gap narrows to 27% and 17%, respectively.

Figure 2.20. **Distribution of youth businesses by performance level**

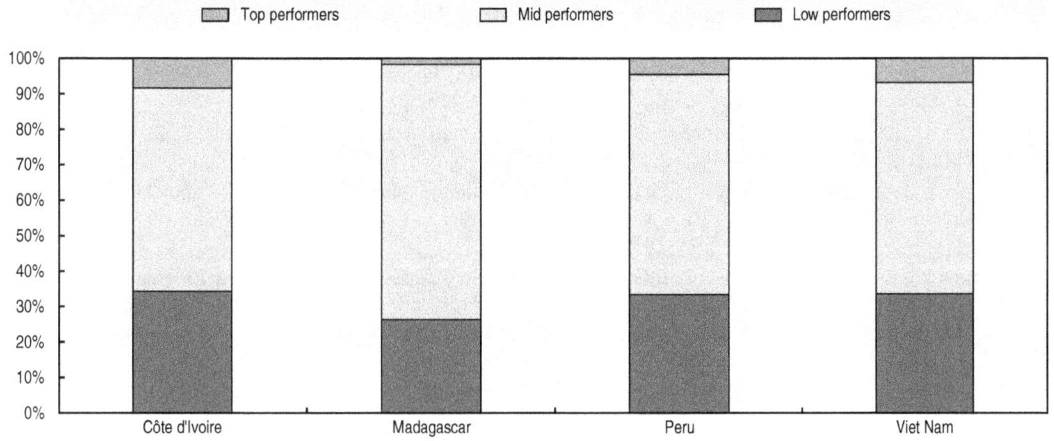

Note: Agriculture excluded. Youth are aged 15-29.
Source: Côte d'Ivoire ENSETE 2014, Madagascar ENEMPSI 2012, Peru ENAHO 2014, and Viet Nam HBIS 2014.

References

AfDB/OECD/UNDP (2017), *African Economic Outlook 2017: Entrepreneurship and Industrialisation*, OECD Publishing, Paris, http://dx.doi.org/10.1787/aeo-2017-en.

AfDB/OECD/UNDP (2015), *African Economic Outlook 2015: Regional Development and Spatial Inclusion*, OECD Publishing, Paris, http://dx.doi.org/10.1787/aeo-2015-en.

AfDB, et al. (2012), *African Economic Outlook 2012: Promoting Youth Employment*, OECD Publishing, Paris, http://dx.doi.org/10.1787/aeo-2012-en.

Arbache, J. S., A. Kolev and E. Filipiak (eds.) (2010), *Gender Disparities in Africa's Labor Market*, World Bank, Washington, DC.

Blattman, C. and S. Dercon (2016), "Occupational choice in early industrializing societies: Experimental evidence on the income and health effects of industrial and entrepreneurial work", *National Bureau of Economic Research Working Paper*, No. 22683, NBER, Cambridge, MA.

Cling, J.-P. (ed.) (2015), *The Informal Economy in Developing Countries*, Routledge, Abingdon, UK, and New York.

Hall, G.H. and H.A. Patrinos (2012), *Indigenous Peoples, Poverty, and Development*, Cambridge University Press, New York.

OECD (2015), *Securing Livelihoods for All: Foresight for Action*, OECD Publishing, Paris. http://dx.doi.org/10.1787/9789264231894-en.

OECD (2013), "Youth entrepreneurship: A background paper for the OECD Centre for Entrepreneurship, SMEs and Local Development", https://www.oecd.org/cfe/leed/youth_bp_finalt.pdf.

Parker, S.C. (2009), *The Economics of Entrepreneurship*, Cambridge University Press, Cambridge, UK.

Nguyen Huu, C. and C.J. Nordman (2014), "Household entrepreneurship and social networks: Panel data evidence from Vietnam", Working paper, UMR DIAL, Paris.

Shane, S.A. (2008), *The Illusions of Entrepreneurship: The Costly Myths that Entrepreneurs, Investors, and Policy Makers Live By*, Yale University Press, New Haven, CT.

United Nations Department of Economic and Social Affairs (2015), "Population facts: Youth population trends and sustainable development", UN DESA, New York.

Chapter 3

Pathways and barriers to entrepreneurial performance

An overwhelmingly large number of youth entrepreneurs in developing countries undertake informal and subsistence activities. How could youth move up the entrepreneurial performance ladder and turn subsistence businesses into performing ones? This central question of the report is addressed in this chapter through cross-country and within-country regression analyses, bringing new empirical evidence for Côte d'Ivoire, Madagascar, Peru and Viet Nam.

A tiny portion of entrepreneurs record high performance levels in terms of profits, employment generation, productivity or other factors. Evidence shows that those who opt voluntarily for entrepreneurship tend to take advantage of market opportunities and start their own business even though they could generate income through other forms of employment (YBI, 2012). In particular, youth who are entrepreneurs out of vocation tend to have the ability to identify good business opportunities and possess better skills to start up a new business and make it grow. These young entrepreneurs constitute a small group, however. An in-depth look at what drives their performance reveals that beyond individual characteristics, important structural conditions lie behind the success factors.

Women and rural dwellers are at risk

Young women are particularly disadvantaged. Being a man is strongly associated with a higher probability of being part of the top performance group. The female disadvantage is particularly pronounced in Peru, where males are nearly 35% more likely than females to be top performers, while they hold an advantage of 25% on average across all countries. Although other traditional determinants of entrepreneurship are controlled for in the analysis, the fact that being a woman is strongly associated with low entrepreneurial performance points to the existence of gender-based barriers to performance that are not captured in the data. These barriers often include women's lack of autonomy in decision making and the additional burden on their time.

Rural dwellers fare clearly worse in terms of business performance. The probability of being a top performer increases by nearly 14% on average for urban dwellers across all countries. The multivariate analysis further shows that the average household size and the share of dependent members steadily increase as business performance level diminishes.

Managerial capital and business skills are key for success

Education significantly increases the chances of better entrepreneurial performance. Overall, upper secondary and tertiary education reduce the likelihood of being a low performer and augment the chances of belonging to the top performing group. The impact of upper secondary education is particularly powerful in Madagascar, where it most strongly decreases the likelihood of low performance, and in Viet Nam, where it most strongly increases the likelihood of top performance. In Côte d'Ivoire, the impact of upper secondary education is actually negative, suggesting that this level of education does not sufficiently endow youth with the necessary skills to move up the entrepreneurial performance ladder. Yet tertiary education in Côte d'Ivoire significantly drives up business performance, as it does in Viet Nam and, to a lesser extent, Peru. In Madagascar, tertiary education does not statistically have a significant impact on business performance, but it is nonetheless more common among top performers.

Managerial capital and business skills are strongly associated with higher performance. Bookkeeping explicitly drives up the likelihood of top performance among youth entrepreneurs, while bringing down the risk of exposure to low performance. Top performers are indeed much more prone to make use of written accounts and are thus more accounting literate, especially in Peru and Viet Nam. Moreover, in Madagascar and Viet Nam, where data are available, top performers exhibit a higher propensity to develop business strategies, although the marginal effect proves to be statistically insignificant for Madagascar. In particular, they more often adopt cost-reduction strategies such as renewing suppliers and limiting manpower costs. In addition, top performers in Viet Nam less often report the need for assistance in product promotion and advertising. In

Madagascar, other practices – active pricing (setting prices in accordance with production costs), shock reaction strategies (to cope with economic strains) and proactivity (active steps to get known among relationships and in the neighbourhood) – do not significantly affect business performance, as these practices are very marginal overall.

Informality weakens youth business performance

The quality of the business environment varies a lot across countries. According to data from the World Bank's *Doing Business Report 2016* (World Bank, 2016), Côte d'Ivoire and Madagascar are among the lowest ranked countries in terms of ease of doing business. In Côte d'Ivoire, starting a business is actually quite easy: procedures, time, cost and minimum capital required are limited, offering favourable conditions to business creation. The problem lies elsewhere, notably in accessing credit and electricity, registering property, enforcing contracts, dealing with warehouse construction permits, paying taxes and other impediments that result in a non-conducive business environment. Madagascar faces similar obstacles, but to a much larger extent. Starting a business is more complicated than in Côte d'Ivoire but, on the positive side, tax regulations and trading across borders are more favourable. In sharp contrast, Viet Nam and especially Peru exhibit more conducive business environments. Peru is one of the leading countries in the world in access to credit, ranking at the 15th position. Its main challenge probably relates to easing business creation by reducing the number of procedures and the time it takes to comply with them. In Viet Nam, the regulatory framework for starting a business is far more complex, with as many as ten different procedures to follow. Viet Nam does worse than Peru in the other domains as well (except in dealing with warehouse construction permits), in particular as regards tax regulations and access to credit. In line with the *Doing Business* data, the World Economic Forum (WEF, 2015) shows that global competitiveness is very low in Côte d'Ivoire, and even lower in Madagascar. By contrast, Peru and especially Viet Nam display much higher levels of competitiveness. The Global Entrepreneurship Monitor (Kelley et al., 2016), which only provides data for Peru and Viet Nam among the sample of countries, reveals that societal values about entrepreneurship are relatively high in these two countries and that a majority of people perceive good opportunities for business creation, especially in Viet Nam. However, the Vietnamese are less confident than Peruvians in their ability to start a business, and have greater fear of business failure. Far fewer Vietnamese than Peruvians say they intend to start a business in the near future.

Informality and low youth business performance go hand in hand. Informality is unambiguously a strong negative driver of youth business performance, especially in Côte d'Ivoire and, above all, in Madagascar, where its impact is significant. In all four countries, informality reduces the chances of being a top performer and, even more, increases the risk of low performance. Madagascar stands out strikingly, with an increased risk of low performance due to informality that reaches 161%. Significant impacts are also observed in the other countries, especially Côte d'Ivoire. However, and in contrast with Viet Nam and in particular Peru, the incidence of informality is barely lower among top performers in Côte d'Ivoire and Madagascar, as almost all of them are running unregistered businesses. In Madagascar, top performers are almost as likely as other young entrepreneurs to express a need for assistance to register their businesses. In contrast, virtually no top performers in Viet Nam express such a need. Viet Nam differs from Madagascar in that its regulatory framework is less complex and burdensome, and thus more conducive to business registration.

Reasons for choosing to be informal include tax avoidance and other factors. Overall, it is uncommon for an entrepreneur to deliberately choose informality (Figure 2.16). Except in Peru, as many as 45% of youth businesses in urban areas choose to be informal. These businesses may opt for informality in order to avoid taxes and regulations. However, very few informal youth businesses in Peru, and almost none in Viet Nam, declare that they are unregistered because of the complexity and cost of registration procedures. In contrast, the regulatory framework in Madagascar prevents a non-negligible number of businesses from registering. This points to the need to simplify procedures and reduce registration costs to make formalisation more attractive. In Viet Nam, the registration process appears to be relatively short and cheap, especially in urban areas. On average, youth can register a business in 11 days, for an approximate cost of VND 300 000 (Vietnamese dong), equivalent to USD 15. Among the perceived advantages of registration, youth businesses mostly mention access to credit, market integration, advertising and reduced corruption. On the last point, it is notable that very few businesses, in particular those owned by youth, say that they have experienced corruption, such as paying bribes, during the registration process. All in all, while simplifying procedures and reducing registration costs is still a valid recommendation in some countries, such as Madagascar, it seems insufficient to spark a large-scale formalisation trend. Spreading information and raising awareness about the gains of formalisation for the enterprises themselves would appear to be indispensable complements.

The sector of activity affects performance differently across countries. Manufacturing seems to offer the highest chances for youth in Peru and Viet Nam to move up the entrepreneurial performance ladder, while in Côte d'Ivoire the dominant sector among top performers is trade. Statistically insignificant results are obtained for Madagascar. In this country, both top and low performers are primarily found in manufacturing, though the former are more evenly distributed across sectors of activity. In Côte d'Ivoire, trade reduces most the likelihood of being a low performer. In Peru and Viet Nam, top performers are primarily located in services and trade, respectively. However, in Peru, both trade and services negatively affect the likelihood of being a low performer, but to a larger extent that of being a top performer, suggesting that manufacturing – which is taken as the sector of reference in the regression analysis – is more rewarding. The same conclusion holds in Viet Nam, where trade and services tend to drive down entrepreneurial performance, though in different ways. A finer disaggregation within each sector of activity across countries reveals that top performers work mainly in the manufacture of food products and clothing, retail trade, and to some extent in land transportation and in hotels and restaurants. Overall, these results highlight the increased opportunities offered by manufacturing in the more economically advanced developing countries, where this sector is generally more developed and less affected by entry barriers. African countries, such as Côte d'Ivoire and Madagascar, need to leverage on its pool of opportunity-driven entrepreneurs for industrialisation and help survival entrepreneurs to transition into the labour market (AfDB/OECD/UNDP, 2017).

Favourable physical operating conditions raise performance

The vast majority of businesses operate in the streets or at home. Only very few have dedicated premises. Working in such a precarious environment as the street is common among young entrepreneurs in Côte d'Ivoire, Madagascar and Peru, both in rural and urban settings (Figure 3.1). In Viet Nam, however, one out of three youth businesses have dedicated premises and less than one-fifth operate in the street, a better situation than that observed for adults in the country.

Figure 3.1. **Type of premises among youth businesses**

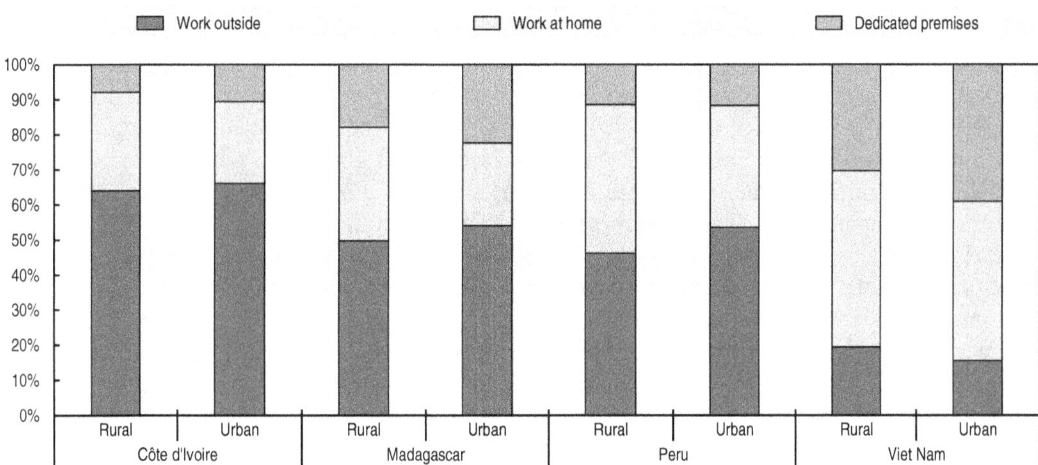

Note: Agriculture excluded. Youth are aged 15-29.
Source: Côte d'Ivoire ENSETE 2014, Madagascar ENEMPSI 2012, Peru ENAHO 2014, and Viet Nam HBIS 2014.

Figure 3.2. **Access to infrastructure and ICTs for production purpose among youth businesses**

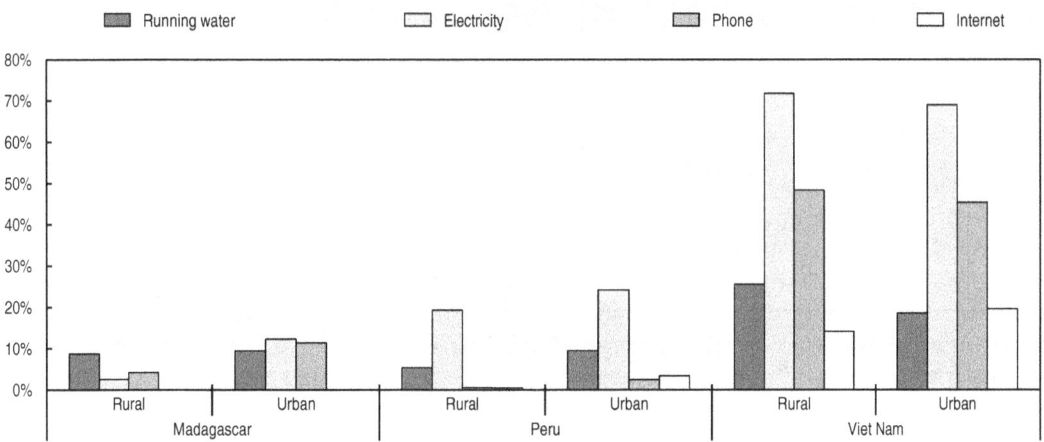

Note: Agriculture excluded. Youth are aged 15-29.
Source: Côte d'Ivoire ENSETE 2014, Madagascar ENEMPSI 2012, Peru ENAHO 2014, and Viet Nam HBIS 2014.

Businesses in Peru and Madagascar lack access to infrastructure and ICT. Access to basic infrastructure services (water and electricity) and, in particular, to information and communication technologies (phone and, to a larger extent, Internet) are lacking for most businesses in Peru and Madagascar (Figure 3.2). Scarce access appears to be more pronounced in rural areas and among young entrepreneurs as compared to adults. In line with previous findings, Viet Nam again stands apart. Businesses in Viet Nam, especially those owned by youth, have much higher access to infrastructure and ICT than businesses in Madagascar and Peru (data not available for Côte d'Ivoire). In Viet Nam, 47% of young entrepreneurs use a phone and 16% use the Internet in their business activity, while very few do so in the other two countries. Access to Internet is a clear correlate and potential driver of innovation. Overall, the results point to the critical importance of improving access to infrastructure, especially in rural parts, and to ICT in order to professionalise youth businesses and foster innovation.

Favourable operating conditions lead to higher youth entrepreneurial performance. Business performance unsurprisingly improves with access to dedicated premises, basic infrastructure services and ICT. Access to dedicated premises shows a markedly positive correlation with increased business performance, especially in Peru. In Côte d'Ivoire, problems upon business creation related to workspace are slightly more often reported among top performers. In contrast, complaints about inadequate premises tend to become less frequent as Vietnamese youth businesses reach higher levels of performance. In Madagascar, youth businesses at upper performance levels less often express the need for assistance in accessing adequate equipment and modern machinery. Access to water and electricity also constitute enabling factors. Madagascar exhibits statistically insignificant marginal effects, but descriptive statistics explicitly show that access to these basic infrastructure services is much more common among top performers. In Viet Nam, surprisingly, only 61% of top performers have access to electricity, compared to 68% of mid performers and 71% of low performers. Business performance improves with access to information and means of communication, and top performers are much more inclined to use a phone in their business activity. In Peru, the impact of telephone use is higher among low performers, suggesting that top performers rely on more sophisticated ICT. In fact, Internet access is a strong driver of higher business performance in Peru, where it is more extensively used among top performers. In Madagascar, where the Internet is almost nonexistent, the very few who have access to it can tremendously increase their chances of moving up the entrepreneurial performance ladder. Internet use has a huge impact on business performance in Madagascar: it decreases the risk of low performance by 157% and increases the probability of top performance by 29%. In Viet Nam, Internet use is far more widespread, making the impact on top performance not so significant.

Access to finance and market integration present major challenges

Access to credit is a primary concern for a large number of youth businesses. Data at hand contain information on self-reported problems and assistance needs of businesses surveyed in Madagascar and Viet Nam. These data reveal that access to credit is a primary concern for a large number of youth businesses in the two countries (Figure 3.3). Ivoirian data also provide information on self-reported problems that arise when starting a business. They confirm recent findings from OECD work on Côte d'Ivoire that stressed the prime importance of financial inclusion and proposed concrete steps to address the lack of funding, which hampers growth (OECD, 2016). (Self-reported data have the advantage of providing insights into a young entrepreneur's perceived problems and needs. It does suffer however from reporting bias, i.e. what entrepreneurs consider as problematic is highly subjective, and some problems, such as their own lack of skills, are less likely to be self-reported.)

A number of factors explain the difficulties of youth in accessing finance. Youth have to deal with a lack of personal savings and resources; inadequate youth-friendly financial products, including micro lending and seed funding; high credit and collateral requirements; excessive restrictions (e.g. age for opening a bank account); low financial literacy; and limited awareness and knowledge of financing opportunities (ILO, 2006; UNCTAD, 2015). Financial institutions are reluctant to lend to youth, who are perceived as risky due to their lack of collateral and experience and their limited credit history with a track record of successful repayment (S4YE, 2015). Consequently, three out of four youths in developing countries rely primarily on meagre personal savings and funding provided by close networks, such as family and friends, to launch their businesses (YBI, 2013).

Figure 3.3. **Main problems expressed by entrepreneurs**

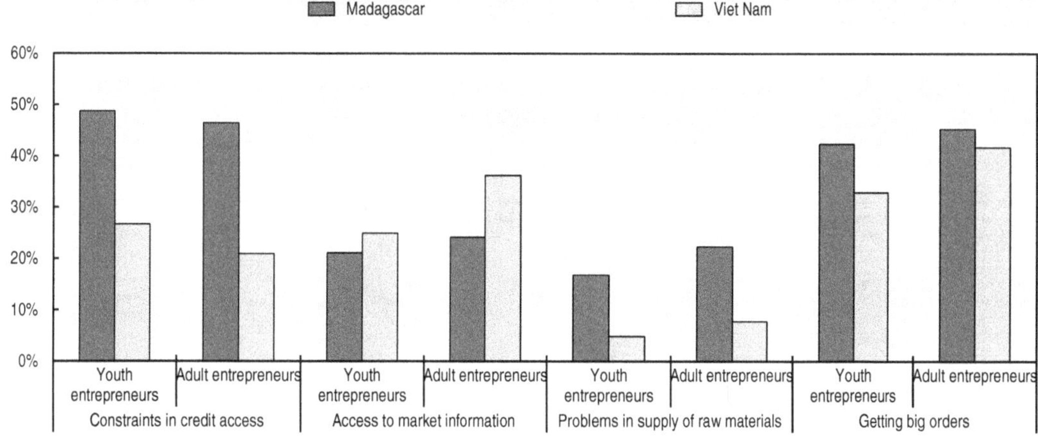

Note: Agriculture excluded. Youth are aged 15-29 and adults 30-64.
Source: Madagascar ENEMPSI 2012 and Viet Nam HBIS 2014.

Youth businesses are poorly integrated to markets. In Madagascar and Viet Nam, for which data on market integration are available, significant proportions of young entrepreneurs express direct need for assistance in accessing market information and big orders, as well as in the supply of raw materials (Figure 3.4). Fewer youth businesses in Madagascar (24%) than in Viet Nam (36%) say they need assistance to access market information. But youth entrepreneurs in Madagascar are more likely to face difficulties in getting big orders (45%) and in dealing with the supply of raw materials (37%) than those in Viet Nam (42% and 25%). Supply of raw materials is a concern of prime importance reported by no less than 22% of Malagasy young entrepreneurs. Selling production is problematic as well for 34% of youth businesses in Viet Nam and 48% in Madagascar.

Figure 3.4. **Main assistance needs expressed by entrepreneurs**

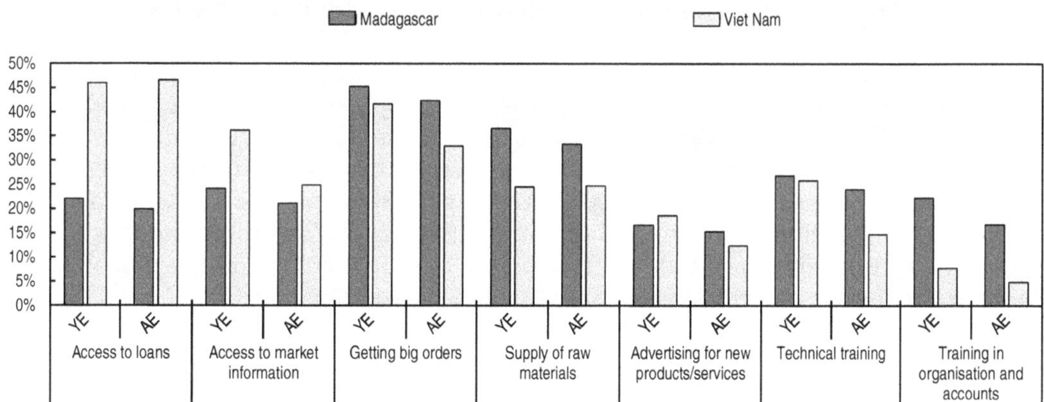

Note: Agriculture excluded. Youth are aged 15-29 and adults 30-64. YE refers to young entrepreneurs and AE to adult entrepreneurs.
Source: Madagascar ENEMPSI 2012, and Viet Nam HBIS 2014.

The vast majority of youth businesses operate in a closed local circuit. Interaction with larger private companies, and in particular with the public sector, is very rare. Youth businesses overwhelmingly buy and sell products or services to individuals and other small businesses, most certainly within a limited geographical area where they operate (Figure 3.5). Competitors are most often restricted to other small local businesses, although in Viet Nam a significant share of youth businesses is found to compete with larger private companies. Moreover, almost no youth businesses in Madagascar or Viet Nam directly export their production, highlighting their lack of ties with global production and value chains. Widening the economic circuit within the domestic market would already represent a great potential for growth for youth businesses.

Figure 3.5. **Market integration: Main suppliers and competitors of youth businesses**

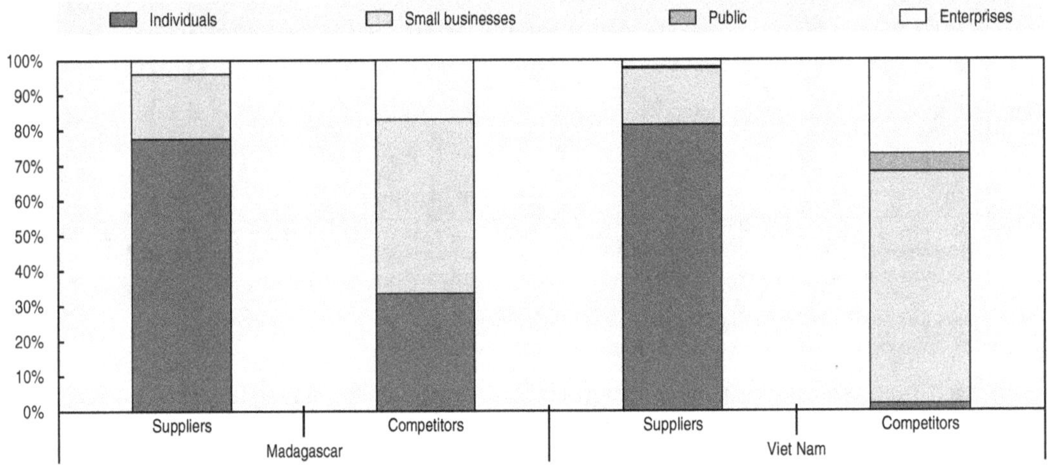

Note: Agriculture excluded. Youth are aged 15-29.
Source: Madagascar ENEMPSI 2012, and Viet Nam HBIS 2014.

Entrepreneurial performance is driven by multiple factors. Bringing to light the differentiated impacts of a number of characteristics on the three entrepreneurial performance levels allows the identification of enabling and disabling factors to higher entrepreneurial performance. The determinants of the probability of belonging to the different youth entrepreneurial performance levels – low, mid and top performers – across the four countries and within each country were analysed using multinomial logit regression models (all models were regressed using sampling weights, except for Madagascar because the likelihood did not converge when using weighted observations). Low performers are taken as the reference group. In Annex A, Table A.1 displays the main individual, household and business characteristics of young entrepreneurs. Marginal effects of the variables included in the models are reported in Table A.2, and young entrepreneurs' expressed problems and assistance needs are shown in Table A.3. Results are reported by entrepreneurial performance level in the four countries under study. Table 3.1 summarises the main findings from the regression analysis. The table identifies enabling and disabling factors to higher entrepreneurial performance among youth, as evidenced by the percentage-point differential in marginal effects on the probability of belonging to the top-performing group vis-à-vis the low-performing one.

Table 3.1. **Enabling and disabling factors to higher entrepreneurial performance among youth**

Differential in marginal effects on the probability of being a top performer vis-à-vis a low performer, in percentage points

Dimension	Factor	All countries	Côte d'Ivoire	Madagascar	Peru	Viet Nam
	Male	24.7	14.2	11.6	34.3	15
Inherent characteristics	Ethnic minorities	N/A	N/A	N/A	N/A	-1.5
Area of residence	Urban	13.6	8.2	12	19.1	13.6
Education (Reference: primary or lower secondary)	Upper secondary	1.7	-3.9	9	7	9.7
	College or tertiary	0.5	4.7	Insignificant	0.7	8.1
	Bookkeeping	12.2	5.5	2.6	8.2	8
	Business strategy	N/A	N/A	Insignificant	N/A	18.2
	Proactivity	N/A	N/A	Insignificant	N/A	N/A
	Shock reaction	N/A	N/A	Insignificant	N/A	N/A
Managerial capital and business skills	Active pricing	N/A	N/A	Insignificant	N/A	N/A
	Innovation	N/A	N/A	N/A	N/A	-37.1
Motivation	Necessity-driven	N/A	N/A	5.2	5.7	-5.4
Informality	Lack of registration	-20.6	-29.3	-160.6	-19.4	-12.2
Sector of activity (Reference: manufacture)	Trade	2.7	1.8	Insignificant	-3.6	-2.5
	Services	2.3	0.2	Insignificant	-3	-6
	Dedicated premises	14.9	12.2	9.5	26.2	11.6
	Water	N/A	N/A	Insignificant	1.2	11.9
	Electricity	N/A	N/A	Insignificant	3.1	-12.5
	Phone	N/A	N/A	15.6	-7	27.8
Access to infrastructure	Internet	N/A	N/A	127.7	15.5	-10.3

Note: Enabling factors are positive numbers, and disabling factors are negative numbers. Marginal effects are given a zero value if they are not statistically significant at a level of at least 10%. Insignificant indicates that neither the marginal effect on the probability of being a top performer nor that of being a low performer is statistically significant at 10% level. N/A means that the factor is not available for the country.
Source: Marginal effects are taken from Annex A Table A.2.

References

AfDB/OECD/UNDP (2017), *African Economic Outlook 2017: Entrepreneurship and Industrialisation,* OECD Publishing, Paris, http://dx.doi.org/10.1787/aeo-2017-en.

International Labour Organization (2006), *Stimulating Youth Entrepreneurship: Barriers and Incentives to Enterprise Start-Ups by Young People,* ILO, Geneva.

Kelley, D., S. Singer and M. Herrington (2016). "Global entrepreneurship monitor: 2015/16 global report", Global Entrepreneurship Research Association, London Business School.

OECD (2016b), *Multi-dimensional Review of Côte d'Ivoire. Volume 3: From Analysis to Action,* OECD Development Pathways, OECD Publishing, Paris, http://dx.doi.org/10.1787/9789264258501-en.

Solutions for Youth Employment (S4YE) (2015), *Toward Solutions for Youth Employment: A 2015 Baseline Report,* ILO, Geneva.

United Nations Conference on Trade and Development (UNCTAD) (2015), *Policy Guide on Youth Entrepreneurship,* UNCTAD, Geneva.

World Bank (2016), *Doing Business 2016: Measuring Regulatory Quality and Efficiency,* World Bank, Washington, DC.

World Economic Forum (2015), *The Global Competitiveness Report 2015-2016,* WEF, Geneva.

Youth Business International (2013), *Generation entrepreneur? The state of global youth entrepreneurship,* YBI, London

Youth Business International (2012), *Youth Entrepreneurship: A Contexts Framework,* YBI, London.

Chapter 4

The way forward: Helping youth entrepreneurs reach their potential

Significant efforts have been deployed in recent years to promote youth entrepreneurship at the national level. Numerous countries now count on policies that support youth entrepreneurship, mainly through entrepreneurship education and skills development in the schooling system, and comprehensive packages offering multiple services such as training, financial support, business advisory services, mentoring and coaching. This chapter looks at policies and programmes that have proven to help young entrepreneurs move up the performance ladder.

Promoting youth entrepreneurship has gained importance on global and national policy agendas. At the international level, a number of initiatives have emerged to support youth entrepreneurship. Fostering youth entrepreneurship is one of the objectives of the Europe 2020 strategy and its Youth on the Move flagship initiative. In addition, employment and entrepreneurship are one of the eight fields of action promoted by the European Union (EU) Youth Strategy (2010-2018). In 2012, the United Nations (UN) called for the development of an action plan called Youth-SWAP to help UN entities work on youth development issues across the UN system. The plan focuses on employment and entrepreneurship as one of its five main thematic areas. Likewise, youth entrepreneurship figures prominently in a 2012 International Labour Organisation (ILO) resolution titled "The youth employment crisis: A call for action" and in the OECD's 2013 Action Plan for Youth. The UN Conference on Trade and Development (UNCTAD) has developed an Entrepreneurship Policy Framework and Implementation Guidance methodology to support policy design for promoting entrepreneurship in developing countries. And the UN Industrial Development Organisation (UNIDO) recently developed an Inclusive Development and Entrepreneurship for All (IDEA) strategy that applies in particular to youth employment and enterprise development. Promoting rural youth employment in developing countries, notably in Africa, also figures very high on the 2016 G20 agenda.

Yet given that a large majority of youth still fail to succeed in entrepreneurship, there is doubt as to how much hope policy makers can place on youth entrepreneurship as a solution to the youth employment challenge. In this context, more attention is needed as to why entrepreneurship is not working as a sustainable solution for gainful employment for most youth, which policies and programmes can help turn subsistence businesses into productive and performing ones, and which types of entrepreneurship promotion intervention are more likely to create decent jobs for youth.

Targeted policy can help young entrepreneurs succeed

Constraints faced by young entrepreneurs confine many to subsistence activities. Evidence from Côte d'Ivoire, Madagascar, Peru and Viet Nam shows that while young entrepreneurs are numerous, there are proportionally fewer than in previous generations in the more economically advanced developing countries. They are less educated than young employees, enter entrepreneurship for the most part as a result of a constrained choice and fare worse in terms of quality of employment. Youth businesses are typically very small – smaller than businesses owned by adults. They deal with disproportionate barriers and operate to a larger extent in more accessible but less rewarding sectors of activity. Young entrepreneurs underperform compared to adults in terms of: business registration; bookkeeping; access to basic infrastructure services and ICT; access to finance; and market integration. Very few make their businesses grow by creating jobs, and the vast majority generate modest profits that fall below the average wage earned by young employees.

Yet a tiny number of young entrepreneurs prove to be successful. Successful youth entrepreneurs are relatively few and exhibit particular characteristics. They are generally well-educated, come from well-off backgrounds and choose this career path out of vocation or to take advantage of a business opportunity. They demonstrate that moving up the entrepreneurial performance ladder, while difficult, is not impossible.

Unlocking youth entrepreneurship potential can boost individuals and society. Evidence on enabling and disabling factors to higher entrepreneurial performance points to the need to invest through a comprehensive integrated approach. Enhancing access to education, managerial capital, enterprise formalisation, infrastructure, finance and market integration has great potential to help youth move up the entrepreneurial performance ladder and turn subsistence businesses into performing ones. It also holds great promise for countries: entrepreneurship can foster job creation, economic growth, poverty alleviation and formalisation of the economy, as indicated by the OECD-EUROSTAT Entrepreneurship Indicators Programme (OECD, 2016a). It also has the potential to spur innovation, increase competition and encourage social cohesion by acting as an integrating mechanism for the disadvantaged and socially excluded (OECD, 2013; OECD/EU, 2012; De Clercq and Honig, 2011). Moreover, entrepreneurship can be an important driver of structural transformation in developing countries by boosting firm creation and reallocation in the modern sector of the economy (UNU-WIDER, 2010), by generating a significant share of new and sustainable jobs, and by contributing to economic diversification (IADB, 2006).

Policy should be targeted to address specific needs. The high heterogeneity observed among youth entrepreneurs calls for policy solutions and interventions that are carefully targeted and tailored to address specific challenges and needs. Different interventions are likely to have different impacts on low and high performing youth entrepreneurs who operate in country-specific contexts. In addition, attention should be paid to addressing the needs of categories of youth entrepreneurs who appear particularly disadvantaged due to inherent characteristics (females and ethnic minorities), family situation (large households with a high share of dependents) or area of residence (rural dwellers). These categories must constitute priority targets for policy action. Policies for youth engaged in subsistence activities should focus on training and redirecting them to transition into the labour market or public works programmes (PWPs). Innovative PWPs can be a promising tool to address employment challenges for the vulnerable youth, if well-combined with training and labour market counselling. Evaluations of public works programmes have been found to be more effective when they involve the community, focus on work other than infrastructure building (e.g. social work) and offer participants skills training to help them find longer-term and sustainable employment (OECD, 2015b).

Impact studies yield useful lessons for boosting entrepreneurship

A number of general conclusions can be drawn from impact evaluation studies. Recent impact evaluations of entrepreneurship programmes in developing countries show that improving business performance and enhancing employment creation is complex. Information on programme effects from rigorously evaluated studies is useful for understanding which type of entrepreneurship intervention is more effective for whom, and for which outcomes. While there is a general lack of quantitative impact assessment of entrepreneurship programmes, in particular for youth, global evidence on programme effectiveness can be obtained from a number of reviews and meta-studies that have tried to estimate causal impacts of an intervention using randomised controlled trials or quasi-experimental techniques (see for instance Kluve et al., 2016; Grimm and Pafhausen, 2015; ILO, 2015; Cho & Honorati, 2013).

Impact evaluations yield lessons specific to each programme. The bulk of empirical evidence on the effectiveness of entrepreneurship programmes covers programmes around policy aims for which it is often possible to identify a counterfactual. These include: i) improving access to finance; ii) enhancing entrepreneurship training; iii) supporting business development services; and iv) promoting the formalisation of businesses. Table 4.1 presents the conclusions from impact evaluations of these programmes. It is important to note that this list is non-exhaustive: other interventions exist that could potentially influence entrepreneurial business performance. There is a scarcity of impact evaluation studies on interventions such as coaching and mentoring, role models and business counselling, and these are consequently not included in the table. It is also difficult to assess nation-wide policies that affect all businesses (such as national reforms to improve the business environment), as experimental evaluation approaches cannot be used. Furthermore, it is hard to control for a range of other factors, such as firm size and country context, making it difficult to disentangle what makes different types of interventions effective.

Table 4.1. **Summary of impact evaluations of entrepreneurship programmes**

Programmes	Overall impact	Caveats
Access to finance (Microcredit schemes, conditional and unconditional cash or in-kind grants, changes to existing credit schemes such as length of repayment)	Mostly effective in creation of new entrepreneurial businesses but not in job survival (i.e. business expansion and job creation). Rather, employment expansion due to microfinance happens mostly in small and medium-sized businesses: those which are already larger, well-established and profitable.	Many of these programmes do not intend to create jobs or are not well designed: loans too small, repayment periods too short, a clear targeting strategy is lacking. Most businesses choose to use capital injections for investments in working capital (e.g. inventories) rather than capital investments (e.g. machines, buildings).
Entrepreneurship training (Business management, accounting, financial literacy, vocational skills)	Many programmes are able to improve business skills, but there is only weak evidence for substantial job creation. Training is more helpful for business creation than for business expansion. Training needs to be intensive: short-term interventions do not have a lasting impact. The combination of finance and training is generally more effective in boosting business creation and expansion than either of them in isolation. However, training and coaching show strong effects irrespective of grants provision.	Micro-entrepreneurs who participated in general business training were more likely to close poorly performing businesses. This suggests that entrepreneurship training enhances the entrepreneurial spirit and makes entrepreneurs think about their business model. Comparing successes and failures suggests that the intensity of treatment combined with the degree of targeting are necessary elements to create an impact.
Business development services (Supplier development, support for environmental audit, provision of working premises)	Business support services contribute effectively to employment generation. Prerequisites are that they be demand-driven, tailor-made and focused.	These services raise the competitiveness of the businesses, which improves business performance and, through this, stimulates expansion. It can take years for these effects to occur.
Business environment (Registration and administrative procedures, business entry reform, information campaigns)	Interventions that promote formalisation yield insignificant or modest positive employment effects (most informal businesses are too small and not profitable enough to take advantage of the potential benefits of formality). Formalisation stimulates market integration, which in turn fosters growth. The decision to formalise is less influenced by the *cost of becoming formal* (time and energy) than by the *costs and benefits of becoming formal* (paying taxes and receiving access to social security). As such, formalisation works in concert with tax breaks and other interventions that make formalisation more beneficial for businesses, and information campaigns without coupled reform seem to lack impact.	The best incentive for formalisation is to offer useful public services, both in terms of simplification of administrative procedures (e.g. one-stop shops) and creating more benefits from formalisation. Forcing businesses to register is unlikely to create employment, as for many entrepreneurial businesses formalisation does not create extra profits, but rather costs. Formalisation has a positive impact on trust in the local governments with which businesses interact. Formalised small businesses show an increased awareness on the importance of paying taxes.

Source: Grimm and Paffhausen, 2015; Kluve et al., 2016; ILO, 2015; Cho and Honorati, 2013.

Financial interventions are most effective in helping new firms get off the ground. They are less effective at spurring business expansion or job creation. Financial interventions include capital injection such as start-up grants, cash and in-kind transfers, and allowances. Other youth-friendly financial products include soft loans, micro-financing and guaranteed loans – including government-backed loans provided through public credit guarantee schemes. These specific lines of credit propose below-market or interest-free loans with less stringent or no capital requirements, but they often rely on strict eligibility criteria to minimise the risk of repayment default. Many of these financial interventions do not aim to create jobs. Loans are often too small, repayment periods too short and the loans are typically used as working capital and not for long-term investments into equipment or buildings. Employment expansion due to microfinance usually occurs in small and medium-sized businesses rather than micro businesses. Thus, those which are already larger, well-established and profitable can benefit the most. Peru, for example, introduced the Start Up Programme in 2012 and, since then, has improved the programme design and increased the budget for start-ups, which now receive resources from the innovation fund (OECD, 2016b). This programme has been expanded, and today it includes seed capital and support for angel-investors networks. The national development bank COFIDE has just made promoting start-ups one of its strategic lines of action, and is looking to promote venture capital and the financial inclusion of new enterprises. Peru has made progress in: (i) strengthening the institutional framework for supporting start-ups, (ii) prioritising social and regional inclusion in its pro-startup policies, (iii) recognising the importance to invest in transforming mind-sets and promoting a culture of entrepreneurship, (iv) modernising support instruments, and (v) streamlining procedures and reforming legislation.

The impact of training programmes on job creation is mixed. Several entrepreneurship training programmes have been developed with a view to raising business management skills, accounting, financial literacy or vocational skills. Evidence shows that training turns out to be more useful for business start-ups than for business expansion (Cho and Honorati, 2013). Moreover, short-term interventions hardly appear to have lasting effects.

Business development services appear to contribute to business expansion. Programmes include a range of interventions, such as supplier development, provision of working premises or support for environmental audit. These services are usually found to raise the competitiveness of the business, thereby improving business performance and stimulating business expansion. An advantage of this type of intervention is that especially small businesses can be helped with rather simple improvements, while larger businesses need more specific and sophisticated support. Important prerequisites are that the development services be demand driven, tailor-made and focused.

Interventions that promote formalisation have limited effect. They tend to yield insignificant or modest positive employment effects, mainly because most informal businesses are too small and not profitable enough to take advantage of the potential benefits of formality. Measures aimed at enterprise formalisation focus on simplifying registration and administrative procedures. Formalisation appears to stimulate market integration, which in turn fosters growth. The decision by an entrepreneur to formalise or not is influenced by the costs and benefits that come with it. Programmes that force firms to formalise have mostly not been effective in stimulating business growth because the benefits coming from formalisation do not sufficiently offset the costs. A better incentive would be to provide more benefits from formalisation, to create public awareness around these benefits and to simplify administrative procedures.

Interventions impact at various levels of the results chain. Finance and training interventions contribute most to business creation, but not necessarily to business survival. Development services, subsidies and support on administrative procedures contribute most strongly to business development and job creation (Grimm and Paffhausen, 2015). Different types of intervention thus have impact at different points in the results chain. Overall, however, it appears easier to boost the creation of entrepreneurial businesses than to expand employment within them.

The most successful programmes target multiple constraints. Capital constraints interact with other constraints. Therefore addressing only capital constraints is often not enough. A combination of finance and training seems to work better than either of these interventions in isolation. As such, the most effective interventions for micro-entrepreneurs in developing countries seem to be those that unlock multiple constraints (Cho and Honorati, 2013).

Youth benefit most from entrepreneurial programmes. The impacts of entrepreneurial interventions are significantly higher for youth in comparison to the general population (Cho et al., 2013). This is especially relevant in countries where youth unemployment is especially high and where youth make up a sizable proportion of the population. Some youth entrepreneurship programmes have been particularly effective in Peru, according to impact evaluations (OECD/CAF/ECLAC, 2016). *Calificación de jóvenes creadores de microempresas* (Certificate of Youth entrepreneurship), *Formación empresarial de la juventud*

(Youth entrepreneurship Programme) and *Projoven Emprendedor* have had positive impacts on employment outcomes. In particular, *Calificación de jóvenes creadores de microempresas* impacted positively psychosocial skills, while *Formación empresarial de la juventud* and *Projoven Emprendedor* boosted firm creation. *Creer para crear*, a start-up programme targeted at youth, led in turn to an increase in earnings among its beneficiaries.

Well-designed entrepreneurship programmes will be more effective

Outcomes are influenced by programme design. Interestingly, many entrepreneurial interventions are not primarily designed to create employment, but rather to increase income stabilisation and poverty reduction. As such, design is an issue in itself (Grimm et al., 2015). Table 4.2 provides a list of policy options in the areas of: access to finance; business support; entrepreneurship training; the business environment; and entrepreneurship awareness. It also provides concrete examples of programmes under each of these domains.

Five factors are key to ensuring programme effectiveness. First, an important lesson from impact evaluation is that adopting a comprehensive, integrated approach is important, since stand-alone programmes are generally found to be less efficient. Entrepreneurship programmes are indeed more successful when they provide integrated packages offering multiple services simultaneously. They do this by combining, for instance, training, business support services and access to finance. Second, programmes need to be country specific and adapted to the local context (level of income or development stage; factor-driven, efficiency-driven or innovation-driven economy; urban versus rural economy). Third, policy formulation must be evidence-based. It should rely on a comprehensive diagnosis of the challenges facing youth entrepreneurs, and their needs, using sound and comparable data. Fourth, all interventions must include a monitoring and evaluation component with SMART indicators (specific, measurable, attainable, relevant, time bound). They must also include comprehensive evaluation processes and feedback mechanisms. Fifth, in order to avoid overlap and reduce inefficiency, it is essential to ensure greater coordination among stakeholders (the state; service providers such entrepreneurship support providers, educational institutions and training centres; the private sector; NGOs).

Financial support is most successful when combined with other interventions. The provision of micro-loans appears to have limited impact and cost-effectiveness. In contrast with injection of capital, microfinance largely remains very expensive for the borrower and restricted to short repayment periods. However, its impact can be substantially increased by providing clients with additional services, especially in terms of training, business assistance and support (European Microfinance Network, 2012). Similarly, guaranteed loans need to be linked with managerial and technical support to be really effective, in particular as regards government-backed loans, which are often not accompanied by additional support. Moreover, government loans need to target beneficiaries better, as they are too often directed towards firms that would have been successful anyway (Hall and Sobel, 2006). Alternative forms of guarantees or collateral must also be considered as a form of credit security in the absence of formal collateral. These alternative forms include the entrepreneur's business plan, educational level, psychometric tests and solidarity group guarantees. Equity financing, mainly through venture capital and angel investors, must be made more accessible to young entrepreneurs, although it is generally confined to innovative start-ups with growth potential. Other forms of funding, such as cooperatives, crowd-funding, mobile money and rotating savings and credit associations (ROSCAs) are of increasing relevance to youth financial inclusion.

Information is another key to success. Beyond youth-friendly financial products, it is equally important to invest in the provision of information and counselling on access to finance, and in improvement of the regulatory framework for start-up finance. Technical assistance in accessing funding can be provided via entrepreneurship centres or incubators. Financial literacy can be promoted trough dedicated programmes. A one-stop-shop service can be made available within banks to assist young entrepreneurs with the application package and issuance of related documents (ILO, 2006; UNCTAD, 2015). Financial products offered to young entrepreneurs must be adequately supervised, for instance through more transparent rating procedures and risk assessment, and the shortening and simplification of lending processes. The minimum capital requirement for starting a business should be reduced, and young people should be encouraged to open bank accounts in order to build a stake in their financial future and enhance their credibility with financial institutions. In addition, young people should be granted tax relief or incentives to increase their personal savings, and hence their chances of amassing sufficient start-up capital.

Reallocation of resources is key to driving up performance

Business development services need to be supported. Resources need to be reallocated away from ineffective programmes and towards the most promising interventions. Business development services have an established track record of contributing effectively to business performance and employment generation. Young people looking to start a business are in need of soft support such as information, advice, coaching and mentoring to help them overcome gaps in their knowledge. An important first step is to make youth more aware of existing business support services. Information can be disseminated through the Internet, government employment service centres and social networks, or by older mentors. One-stop shops, either physical or electronic online portals, are of particular relevance since they allow youth to access a number of services and to complete and comply with all formalities, including business registration, at one location for a fixed fee. It can also be useful to establish youth-specific enterprise centres or agencies providing integrated packages of services covering, for instance, skills training, business counselling and mentoring, and access to finance.

Business assistance programmes need adequate resources. Medium- to long-term assistance is key to raising business survival rates. Yet business development assistance programmes are too often short-term, with continued assistance rarely extending beyond the first year of business operation (OECD, 2015a; OECD, 2015b). Adequate resources are needed to ensure that business assistance services remain available in the medium to long term. An important challenge facing young entrepreneurs, in particular during the business start-up phase, is their isolation due to a lack of business connections. Mentoring, especially through formal means under dedicated programmes, must be encouraged so as to provide young entrepreneurs with advice and guidance from experienced professionals. Initiatives that are particularly useful in bringing young people together to exchange ideas and share experiences include business clubs, chambers of commerce, platforms created by enterprises and financial institutions, and youth-led networks. These initiatives provide young entrepreneurs with opportunities to enlarge their networks, meet investors and gain expertise by connecting with established businesses and successful entrepreneurs. Moreover, it is worth developing clusters, in particular within or near academic institutions, that link young entrepreneurs with financial investors. Such clusters could also provide access to technology and innovation and facilitate knowledge exchange, product promotion and research commercialisation.

Investment in business incubators holds great promise. Business incubators, although often restricted to highly innovative start-ups, provide a good opportunity for young entrepreneurs to group together, access physical working space and benefit from a spectrum of resources and services. These range from mentoring and coaching to administrative services, technical support and legal advice on intellectual property and financing sources. Alternatively, mini-incubators providing shared workspaces but limited resources and services can be developed. Highly innovative start-ups, operating in particular in the digital economy, can be integrated into business accelerators that provide short but intense programmes meant to turn good ideas into new and scalable businesses. Given the importance of favourable physical operating conditions in driving up youth entrepreneurship performance, business infrastructure can also be improved through co-shared working hubs and the provision of basic service equipment.

Guiding principles include a focus on education

Comprehensive entrepreneurship education is needed in schools. The formal schooling system must integrate comprehensive entrepreneurship education into the national curriculum at all levels. Comprehensive curricula need to be developed that provide young people with different sets of competencies, including technical, non-cognitive and life skills as well as entrepreneurial behaviours (OECD/EU, 2012). At the primary level, it is important: to raise awareness about entrepreneurship as a career opportunity for adult life; to develop skills, knowledge and attitudes that are conducive to entrepreneurial behaviour; to promote entrepreneurship through extracurricular activities; and to develop experiential and learning-by-doing methodologies. At the secondary level, efforts must be deployed: to encourage more interactive, hands-on and experiential teaching methods (e.g. team-based activities, role playing, simulations and games); to promote entrepreneurship through diverse extracurricular activities; to integrate entrepreneurship into the curriculum as an optional course or an after-school activity; and to promote the use of technology, especially the Internet. At the tertiary level, it is essential: to develop effective curricula that provide students with the basic skills for starting and operating a business, including basic accounting; to create entrepreneurship schools and integrate the teaching of entrepreneurship into traditional subject matter; to establish, within universities, entrepreneurship centres that engage in training, R&D, consultancy and information dissemination, and that provide follow-up services to students; and to facilitate networking and exchange among universities in order to increase the spread and use of innovative pedagogies and teaching materials in entrepreneurship education.

Business development skills need greater attention in vocational training. New methods of assessment and accreditation of vocational schools must be developed, and separate schools for entrepreneurship development – that are affiliated with, but distinct from, vocational schools – must be created, allowing students simultaneously to develop entrepreneurial and vocational skills. Furthermore, entrepreneurs and private sector firms must be more effectively engaged, in particular in supplying curriculum guidelines and materials. There is also a need to enhance the training of educators and trainers so as to enable them to use innovative, learner-centred and active learning methods conducive to entrepreneurship training. Networks of trainers must be promoted by creating mechanisms that facilitate the exchange of good practices and sharing of resources. Various forms of public-private cooperation must be developed (e.g. networks, shared facilities, apprenticeships). Last but not least, training programmes must be better targeted in order to cover disadvantaged and under-represented groups; equip young entrepreneurs with more practical skills; develop tailored training online through web-based platforms. They should partner with diverse actors, including development agencies, NGOs, communities and local business organisations (e.g. sponsorship, involvement of voluntary mentors), and should be properly evaluated in order to be able to assess and improve their effectiveness.

Youth entrepreneurship spirit should be promoted through success stories and role models. The talent of young entrepreneurs deserves to be highlighted. This may be done by organising conferences and highly visible summits, and by supporting youth entrepreneurship competitions, awards and events to raise the profile of young entrepreneurs and create awareness about entrepreneurship. The development of networks of young entrepreneurs must be encouraged. This includes peer networks grouping youth entrepreneurship organisations, business associations, youth-led organisations and other stakeholders. Entrepreneurship potential can also be promoted via knowledge exchange between established businesses and aspiring young entrepreneurs. Cross-country networks can work as a driver of global knowledge sharing and business performance. Ultimately, young entrepreneurs must be given more visibility. To this end, media and other communication tools and platforms can be used, in particular to promote role models. Outreach activities must be put in place, through the mass media or by youth outreach workers, to encourage disadvantaged youth in particular to consider self-employment and entrepreneurship as both an option and an opportunity.

Administrative procedures need to be simplified. This can be achieved by making business registration quicker and less expensive, simplifying tax filing requirements and accounting methods, and reviewing bankruptcy laws to make them more tolerant of risk taking and business failure. Tax regimes must be rendered more supportive, for instance by lowering tax rates or introducing tax and social contribution exemptions for young entrepreneurs. In addition, the business regulatory environment needs to be more predictable. Frequent changes in business regulations must be avoided, and young entrepreneurs must be informed early enough when they occur. Competition law must be made more effective and property protection guaranteed. The regulatory framework needs to be more transparent, with clear rules on compliance and insolvency and effective mechanisms for resolving disputes. The issue of corruption must be addressed by implementing reforms aiming at increased transparency and accountability, including in the provision of financial services. Finally, it is important to provide young entrepreneurs with assistance and advice on regulatory matters, for instance regarding taxes and administrative processes related to business registration. Information on procedures and ongoing changes in the regulatory framework must be better disseminated, through entrepreneurship centres, seminars, youth-friendly platforms such as social media and young entrepreneurs' networks, and via information campaigns. Since lack of knowledge about the regulatory framework is a strong driver of informality, interventions aiming at providing information can substantially foster formalisation.

A correct mix of incentives and sanctions is needed to encourage formalisation. Governments often adopt formalisation policies in an attempt to counteract the loss of tax revenue associated with informality. Recent studies have found converging evidence that enterprises also gain by entering the formal sector (McKenzie and Sakho, 2010; Fajnzylber et al., 2011; Rand and Torm, 2012; Demenet et al., 2016). Formalisation benefits businesses by changing their operating conditions. Released from the constraints of informality, they can access better equipment, increase their scale of operation and operate in a more competitive environment. However, not all enterprises benefit in the same way, and among the smallest and most precarious production units, the effect of formalisation is still unclear. Rather than strict enforcement of formality, which is often socially costly and rarely efficient, the way to go is probably to encourage registration, especially through fiscal incentives, awareness-raising campaigns, simplification of business regulations, and business advice and training for informal entrepreneurs (OECD/EU, 2015). Along these lines, there is also a need to reduce the incentives for remaining informal. This demands careful monitoring of the impact of taxes and social contributions.

A holistic, long-term vision is required to foster value chain development. Although evidence is still scarce on the impact of value chain interventions, fostering integration into local and global value chains can potentially have a large impact on employment creation and job quality. One important area of action at the national level is to link entrepreneurs to multinational enterprises and global value chains by attracting foreign direct investment and promoting supplier development. At the sub-national level, greater emphasis should be devoted to supporting local value chains by improving the functioning and the integration of local markets.

Table 4.2. **Policy options and examples of entrepreneurship programmes in developing countries**

Policy area	Policy options	Example of entrepreneurship programmes
Improving access to finance	**Provision of grants and free money: physical capital injection** • Start-up grants. • Investment and working capital financing through cash and in-kind transfers. • Temporary allowances to cover living expenses. • Prizes and awards as a source of "free" start-up capital. • National funds to subsidise youth entrepreneurship.	• SERCOTEC's Seed Capital Programme (SCP) in Chile. • BRAC's multifaceted programme on entrepreneurship for the poor. • UNCDF's YouthStart programme in Burkina Faso, Ethiopia, Malawi, Rwanda, Togo, Uganda, Senegal, and Democratic Republic of Congo. • CYFI's School Bank in India.
	Facilitating debt financing: loans and specific lines of credit • Soft-loan approach: provision of no- or low-interest loans (no collateral requirements but strict eligibility criteria). • Micro-financing: smaller loans with lower or interest-free rates and less stringent or no collateral requirements. • Guaranteed loans, including public credit guarantee schemes (government-backed loans). • Alternative forms of guarantee/collateral: business plan, psychometric tests to assess risks of repayment default, social capital mechanisms (solidarity group guarantees).	• Bharatiya Yuva Shakti Trust (BYST) in India. • Formación Empresarial De La Juventud in Peru. • Commonwealth Youth Credit Initiative (CYCI). • Projoven Emprendedor in Peru. • Banhcafe Foundation in Honduras. • Creer para Crear in Peru. • Fundación Impulsar in Argentina. • Mutual EMPRETEC Guarantee Association in Ghana. • Nacional Financiera (NAFIN) in Mexico. • Regional Programme for Youth Employment and Social Cohesion (YERP) in Guinea. • Harvard Entrepreneurial Finance Lab. • Spandana's microfinance programme in India. • Akhuwat's interest-free loans financed through civil society in Pakistan.
	Equity financing possibilities for young entrepreneurs • Venture capital: equity investments to support pre-launch, launch and early stages of business development (for innovative start-ups with growth potential). • Angel investors and networks: capital provided, in particular to high growth start-ups, usually in exchange of an equity stake (fills the gap between money from close networks and venture capital). • Impact investment: fundraising among individuals, foundations, NGOs and capital markets to support job creation and service provision for marginalised groups.	• Business Partners International (BPI) SME Fund in Kenya. • African venture GroFin.

Table 4.2. **Policy options and examples of entrepreneurship programmes in developing countries** *(cont.)*

Policy area	Policy options	Example of entrepreneurship programmes
Improving access to finance	**Other forms of funding** • Cooperatives: wide range of financial products offered, mixing both formal and informal guarantees. People can borrow up to a certain level of their savings; parents can act as guarantors of young people's loans. (Poorly governed schemes, characterised by lack of accountability, ineffective supervision and weak standards, put their clients at risk). • Crowd-funding: funds raised in small amounts from other individuals or groups, via the Internet and, increasingly, using mobile technology and social media. (Potential in developing countries yet to be realised due to underdeveloped infrastructure to support the platform). • Mobile money: to facilitate access to financial services, and hence promote financial inclusion, of small and unbanked businesses, especially in rural areas. (Appropriate regulatory frameworks required, including oversight mechanisms). • Rotating savings and credit associations (ROSCAs): Regular deposits to a collective informal savings pot where each participant in turn withdraws the full savings amount. This method requires no external resources such as loans or transfers; neither does it require any public administrative procedure.	• KIVA online lending platform (based in the United States but serving borrowers in more than 80 countries). • Safaricom's M-Pesa mobile money and M-Shwari savings and loans in Kenya. • Saving for Change ROSCA programme in Mali.
	Information and counselling on access to finance and funding • Technical assistance to access funding: e.g. entrepreneurship centres, incubators. • Promoting financial literacy: programmes can be provided, for instance, by financial institutions or NGOs. • One-stop shop service: to be provided by banks to assist young entrepreneurs with the application package and issuance of related documents.	• Reserve Bank Financial Literacy project in India • Equity Bank's vans in Kenya (making banking services more accessible to rural areas).
	Improving the regulatory environment for start-up finance • Adequate supervision of financial products: transparent rating procedures and risk assessment, shortening and simplification of lending procedures, verification and differentiation of lending and credit scoring criteria taking into account real conditions of entrepreneurs, realistic assessment of business viability and associated risks to avoid getting entrepreneurs into unserviceable debt. • Minimum capital requirement: reduce the threshold to start a business. • Encourage youth to open bank accounts: offer them the opportunity to open and manage a savings account to enhance their credibility with financial institutions, by lowering the age limit (under 16) and instituting a child proxy system to allow parents to open an account on their behalf. • Tax regulations: provide youth with tax relief or incentives to increase their personal savings and subsequently their chances of reaching sufficient start-up capital.	• South African National Credit Regulator. • Pioneer Status (PS) and Investment Tax Allowance (ITA) in Malaysia.

Table 4.2. **Policy options and examples of entrepreneurship programmes in developing countries** (cont.)

Policy area	Policy options	Example of entrepreneurship programmes
Business assistance and support	**Providing information, advice and counselling** • Raise awareness: make youth more aware of existing business support services. • Information dissemination: through the Internet, government employment service centres, youth social networks or older mentors. • One-stop shops: physical or electronic online portals as a tool enabling young entrepreneurs to complete and comply with all formalities at one location for a fixed fee. • Youth enterprise centres or agencies: provide youth with integrated packages of one-stop shop solutions, including basic skills training, business counselling and mentoring, brokering services and access to funds. Can also provide on-the-job business skills training (e.g. business plan preparation, start-up administration, project formulation, planning, financing options, accountancy, taxation, marketing and employment law).	• Synapse Centre in Senegal. • Atyrau Business Advisory Center in Kazakhstan. • Programa Juventud, Empleo y Migración in Costa Rica
	Building business networks • Business mentoring: encourage informal mentoring, which develops on its own between partners, or formal mentoring through programmes (assigned relationships, often associated with organisational mentoring programmes designed to provide young entrepreneurs with informal advice and guidance from experienced professionals). • Business networks platforms: business clubs (to develop business ideas and raise opportunities to enlarge networks and meet investors), chambers of commerce and platforms created by enterprises and financial institutions (to connect with successful entrepreneurs at local and international levels, and gain expertise), youth-led networks (important role in linking young entrepreneurs with established businesses). • Developing clusters: link young entrepreneurs to financial investors, and help spread technology and innovation by facilitating knowledge exchange, product promotion and research commercialisation. (Clusters often located in close proximity to academic institutions so as to benefit from their highly skilled human resources). • Business incubators: provision of physical working space where young entrepreneurs group together and benefit from a wide range of resources and services (management coaching, mentoring, business plan preparation, administrative services, technical support, business networking and access to an experienced network of experts, legal advice on intellectual property and sources of financing). Often restricted to highly innovative start-ups. • Alternative business incubator models: mini-incubators such as shared workspace models (workspace, ICT infrastructure, little financial subsidies, media promotion, mentoring and consulting for a limited period of time). • Business accelerators: time-bound and intense programmes that support digital start-ups by turning good ideas into new, scalable digital businesses.	• Honey Bee Network in India. • Red de Emprendedores Bavaria in Colombia. • Youth Business International (YBI). • Business Incubator Facility of the Rwanda's Kigali Institute of Science and Technology. • Espace d'entreprendre in Tunisia. • Alan Grey Foundation and Raizcorp in South Africa.

Table 4.2. **Policy options and examples of entrepreneurship programmes in developing countries** (cont.)

Policy area	Policy options	Example of entrepreneurship programmes
Business assistance and support	**Improving business infrastructures** • Co-shared working hubs: structures that allow entrepreneurs to convene and discuss new ideas without having to rent an office space. • Provision/sharing of basic service equipment: e.g. computers, cars, transporters. Can be of valuable support for young entrepreneurs. Larger companies or public service institutions could provide young entrepreneurs with service equipment they do no need any more or that they are exchanging or modernising.	• Autoempleo Juvenil in Oaxaca, Mexico. • Casablanca Technopark Incubation Centre in Morocco
Enhancing entrepreneurship education and business skills	**Entrepreneurship formal education** • General recommendations: offer comprehensive entrepreneurship education into national curriculum at all formal education system levels; develop comprehensive curricula on technical, non-cognitive and life skills and on entrepreneurial behaviours (e.g. confidence, flexibility, negotiation, opportunity seeking, resilience, leadership, network building, risk-orientation); improve/adapt training for educators and trainers to equip them with innovative, learner-centred and active learning methods conducive to entrepreneurship training; promote networks of trainers (mechanisms to facilitate good practices exchange and resource sharing); develop public/private cooperation (e.g. networks, shared-facilities, apprenticeships). • Primary education: increase awareness of entrepreneurship as a career opportunity; develop a set of knowledge, skills and attitudes conducive to entrepreneurial behaviour; promote entrepreneurship through extracurricular activities (e.g. invite local entrepreneurs to visit classrooms or take students to local businesses to get acquainted with entrepreneurial experiences); promote experiential and learning-by-doing methodologies. • Secondary education: encourage more interactive, hands-on and experiential teaching methods, such as team-based activities, role playing, simulations, games, and short-term business start-ups (e.g. business set-up simulation, entrepreneurship competitions); promote entrepreneurship through extra-curricular activities; integrate entrepreneurship throughout the curriculum as an optional course or an after-school activity; promote the use of technology, especially Internet; introduce mandatory accountancy training. • Tertiary education: develop effective curricula to provide students with the basic skills for starting and operating a business (theoretical knowledge and implementation skills); create entrepreneurship schools and/or integrate entrepreneurship within traditional subject teaching; establish centres for entrepreneurship within universities to engage in training, R&D, consultancy, information dissemination, and provide follow-up services to students; facilitate networking and exchange among universities (increase the spread and use of innovative pedagogies and teaching materials in entrepreneurship education).	• Entrepreneurial Pedagogy Methodology (EPM) in Brazil. • Curricula reform in Rwanda. • Singapore Management University. • University of Zambia's, Technology Development and Advisory Unit. • Bright China Foundation. • Instituto Peruano de Acción Empresarial.
	Vocational training • Curricula: include business development skills and real-world knowledge and focus less on the formal business plan. • Entrepreneurship schools: create separate schools for entrepreneurship development that are affiliated but distinct from vocational schools (to learn simultaneously entrepreneurial and vocational skills). • Vocational schools: develop new methods of assessment and accreditation of vocational schools. • Link with entrepreneurs and private sector: create more effective engagement with entrepreneurs, and engage private sector firms to supply curriculum guidelines and materials.	• Kenya Youth Training and Employment Creation Project (KYTEC). • Know About Business (KAB) programme (TVET). • Rule-of-thumb training in Dominican Republic.

Table 4.2. **Policy options and examples of entrepreneurship programmes in developing countries** (cont.)

Policy area	Policy options	Example of entrepreneurship programmes
Enhancing entrepreneurship education and business skills	**Training programmes** • Disadvantaged and under-represented groups: design better targeted programmes for these groups of entrepreneurs. • Practical skills: equip young entrepreneurs with more practical skills such as opportunity recognition, business planning and running pilot businesses, soft skills (e.g. sense of initiative, creativity, autonomy, teamwork). • Web-based platforms: develop tailored training online through web-based platforms. • Partnerships: partnering with diverse actors, including development agencies, NGOs, communities and local business organisations to promote entrepreneurship. • Programme evaluation: promote better evaluation of programmes to assess and improve their effectiveness.	• Economic Empowerment of Adolescent Girls (EPAG) project in Liberia. • Start and Improve Your Business (SIYB). • Calificación de Jóvenes Creadores De Microempresas in Peru. • Chile Joven Programme (I and II). • Programa Jóvenes Rurales Emprendedores del SENA in Colombia.
Optimising the regulatory framework	**Simplification and alleviation of administrative procedures** • Facilitate business registration procedures: benchmark time and cost of starting a business; review and simplify regulatory requirements (e.g. licensing procedures, administrative requirements); promote online business registration and ICT-based procedures for business registration and reporting; create a one-stop-shop to allow entrepreneurs to complete all registration procedures at one location for a fixed fee. • Simplify tax filling requirements: introduce electronic tax statement with no waiting in line, shorter transaction times and 24 hours a day availability (more difficult to implement in developing countries). • Simplify accounting methods: especially when determining entrepreneurs' tax liability so they can deploy less effort on complex accounting regulations. • Review bankruptcy laws: to make young entrepreneurs more tolerant to risk-taking and business failure; and reduce the administration cost of the process (need to find the right balance between a bankruptcy process that discourages fraud and policies that encourage youth to set up a business). • Make tax regimes more supportive: lower tax rates or grant a period of tax exemptions and reduce social contributions for young entrepreneurs. • Remove trade barriers: to foster young entrepreneurs' integration into global value chains. (Increased competition resulting from trade liberalisation can leave aside many young entrepreneurs who are not resourceful enough to adapt to a more competitive environment). **Making business regulatory environment more predictable** • Changes in business regulation: avoid frequent changes and inform young entrepreneurs early enough about such changes (e.g. provision of a schedule for implementation of relevant policy changes). • Competition law: make competition law more effective and guarantee property protection (property rights, copyright, patent and trademark regulations). • Regulatory framework: make regulatory framework more transparent with clear rules on compliance and insolvency and effective mechanisms for resolving disputes. • Corruption: implement reforms aiming at increased transparency and accountability, including in the provision of financial services.	• One Stop Shop (OSS) in Indonesia. • One-stop-shop system in the FYR of Macedonia. • Bangladesh Better Business Forum. • Millennium Challenge Corporation Threshold Programme in Albania. • New insolvency law in Latvia. • Business Regulatory Reform Unit in Kenya. • Access to Government Procurement Opportunities (AGPO) in Kenya. • Improving contract enforcement in Zambia.

Table 4.2. **Policy options and examples of entrepreneurship programmes in developing countries** *(cont.)*

Policy area	Policy options	Example of entrepreneurship programmes
Optimising the regulatory framework	**Providing assistance and advice on regulatory issues** • Taxes: assist young entrepreneurs on tax issues (e.g. keeping records, overview of tax issues). • Administrative processes: provide a step-by-step checklist of administrative processes during the registration phase. • Information dissemination: disseminate information on procedures and ongoing changes in the regulatory environment, through entrepreneurship centres, seminars, youth-friendly platforms (e.g. social media, young entrepreneurs' networks), and by carrying out informational campaigns on regulatory issues. Lack of knowledge about the regulatory framework, and in particular business registration, is an important driver of informality among young entrepreneurs. Therefore policies targeted at providing information can substantially foster formalisation.	• Guidance on regulatory requirement by the Department of Planning and Investment in Viet Nam. • Information distribution (Booklet Intervention) in Brazil. • SIMPLES (Integrated System for the Payment of Taxes and Social Security Contributions for Micro and Small Enterprises) in Brazil.
Promoting awareness about entrepreneurship	**Highlighting the talent of young entrepreneurs** • Conferences and highly visible summits: organise such events to highlight the talent of young entrepreneurs. • Competitions, awards and events: to raise the profile of young entrepreneurs and create awareness about entrepreneurship. **Promoting entrepreneurship networks to support the development of an entrepreneurial culture** • Young entrepreneurs' and peer networks: encourage the development of networks that gather young entrepreneurs' organisations, business associations, youth-led organisations as well as stakeholders in education, business sector, and NGO community. • Promote cross-country networks: as a driver of global knowledge sharing and business performance. • Promote knowledge exchange: between established businesses and aspiring young entrepreneurs. **Providing visibility to young entrepreneurs** • Media and other communication tools and platforms: to educate, inform and motivate young people (television, radio and the press; serial drama and TV shows; digital media – websites and social media platforms). • Promote role models: with successful entrepreneurs delivering an image of independence, success and achievement through media campaigns. • Disadvantaged youth: outreach activities through mass media or youth outreach workers to encourage disadvantaged youth to consider self-employment as an option and opportunity.	• Commonwealth-Asia Alliance of Young Entrepreneurs. • Berytech Incubation Awards in Lebanon. • Action Community for Entrepreneurship (ACE) in Singapore. • Start-up Programme in Chile. • TV show El Mashrou3 in Egypt.

References

Cho, Y. and M. Honorati (2013), "Entrepreneurship programs in developing countries: A meta regression analysis," World Bank, Washington, DC.

De Clercq, D. and B. Honig, B. (2011), "Entrepreneurship as an integrating mechanism for disadvantaged persons", in *Entrepreneurship & Regional Development*, Vol. 23/5-6, pp. 353–372.

Demenet, A., M. Razafindrakoto and F. Roubaud (2016), "Do informal businesses gain from registration and how? Panel data evidence from Vietnam", in *World Development*, Vol. 84, pp. 326–341, Elsevier, Amsterdam.

European Microfinance Network (2012), "EMN study for youth entrepreneurship", *EMN Research Papers*, Brussels.

Fajnzylber, P., W.F. Maloney and G.V. Montes-Rojas, (2011), "Does formality improve micro-firm performance? Evidence from the Brazilian SIMPLES program", in *Journal of Development Economics*, Vol. 94/2, pp. 262–276, Elsevier, Amsterdam.

Grimm, M. and A.L. Paffhausen (2015), "Do interventions targeted at micro-entrepreneurs and small and medium-sized firms create jobs? A systematic review of the evidence for low and middle income countries", in *Labour Economics*, Vol. 32 (2015), pp. 67–85, Elsevier, Amsterdam.

Hall, J.C. and R.S. Sobel (2006), *Public Policy and Entrepreneurship*, Center for Applied Economics, University of Kansas School of Business, Lawrence, Kansas.

Inter-American Development Bank (2006), *Is Youth Entrepreneurship a Necessity or an Opportunity? A First Exploration of Household and New Enterprise Surveys in Latin America*, IADB, Washington, DC.

International Labour Organisation (2015), *Small and medium-sized enterprises and decent and prpoductive employment creation*, ILO, Geneva.

International Labour Organization (2006), *Stimulating Youth Entrepreneurship: Barriers and Incentives to Enterprise Start-Ups by Young People*, ILO, Geneva.

Kluve, J., S. Puerto, D.M. Robalino, J. Romero, J. Stöterau, F. Weidenkaff and M. Witte (2016), *Interventions to Improve the Labour Market Outcomes of Youth: A Systematic Review of Training, Entrepreneurship Promotion, Employment Services and Subsidized Employment Interventions*, ILO.

McKenzie, D. and Y.S. Sakho (2010), "Does it pay firms to register for taxes? The impact of formality on firm profitability," in *Journal of Development Economics*, Vol. 91/1, pp. 15–24, Elsevier, Amsterdam.

OECD (2016a), *Entrepreneurship at a Glance 2016*, OECD Publishing, Paris. http://dx.doi.org/10.1787/entrepreneur_aag-2016-en

OECD (2016b), *Start-up Latin America 2016: Building an Innovative Future*, OECD Publishing, Paris. DOI: http://dx.doi.org/10.1787/9789264265660-en

OECD (2015a), *Skills Outlook 2015*, OECD Publishing, Paris, http://www.oecd-ilibrary.org/education/oecd-skills-outlook-2015_9789264234178-en.

OECD (2015b), *Investing in Youth: Tunisia*, OECD Publishing, Paris, http://www.oecd-ilibrary.org/social-issues-migration-health/investing-in-youth-tunisia_9789264226470-en

OECD (2013), *Policy Brief on Social Entrepreneurship: Entrepreneurial Activities in Europe*, https://www.oecd.org/cfe/leed/Social%20entrepreneurship%20policy%20brief%20EN_FINAL.pdf.

OECD/CAF/ECLAC (2016), *Latin American Economic Outlook 2017: Youth, Skills and Entrepreneurship*, OECD Publishing, Paris. http://dx.doi.org/10.1787/leo-2017-en

OECD/EU (2015), "Entrepreneurial Activities in Europe: Informal Entrepreneurship", *OECD Employment Policy Papers*, No. 8, OECD Publishing, Paris, http://dx.doi.org/10.1787/5jrtpbxspw7k-en.

OECD/EU (2012), "Entrepreneurial Activities in Europe: Youth Entrepreneurship", *OECD Employment Policy Papers*, No. 1, OECD Publishing, Paris, http://dx.doi.org/10.1787/5jxrcmlf2f27-en.

Rand, J. and N. Torm (2012), "The Benefits of formalization: Evidence from Vietnamese manufacturing SMEs", in *World Development*, Vol. 40/5, pp. 983–998.

United Nations Conference on Trade and Development (UNCTAD) (2015), *Policy Guide on Youth Entrepreneurship*, UNCTAD, Geneva.

United Nations University/ World Institute for Development Economics Research (2010), "Promoting entrepreneurship in developing countries: Policy challenges", UNU, Helsinki.

Annex A. Youth entrepreneurial characteristics by performance level

Table A.1. **Main individual, household and business characteristics of young entrepreneurs by performance level**

	Viet Nam			Madagascar			Côte d'Ivoire			Peru		
	Top	Middle	Low	Top	Middle	Low	Top	Middle	Low	Top	Middle	Low
Distribution by performance level	6.8%	59.6%	33.6%	1.7%	72.0%	26.3%	8.4%	57.3%	34.3%	4.5%	62.1%	33.3%
Education level												
Primary or lower secondary	3.2%	20.6%	17.6%	29.2%	51.8%	65.6%	65.4%	72.6%	73.1%	1.2%	8.8%	12.9%
Upper secondary	62.8%	51.3%	58.6%	58.0%	42.7%	33.4%	28.5%	23.4%	24.0%	54.5%	54.9%	49.4%
College or tertiary	33.9%	28.2%	23.8%	12.8%	5.5%	1.0%	6.2%	4.0%	3.0%	44.3%	36.2%	37.7%
Individual characteristics												
Age	25.99	26.40	25.16	26.34	24.12	22.40	25.27	24.77	24.19	25.68	24.32	23.04
Male	50.8%	61.6%	33.1%	47.1%	46.9%	28.3%	56.7%	36.0%	28.4%	77.3%	67.2%	33.3%
Ethnic minorities	11.5%	8.6%	15.7%	n.a	n.a	n.a	16.2%	23.1%	20.8%	10.8%	16.3%	18.8%
Married	58.2%	78.0%	61.2%	77.9%	69.6%	61.7%	51.5%	60.3%	58.1%	44.4%	40.4%	36.5%
Household size	04.42	4.86	4.09	3.11	3.60	4.47	4.13	4.39	4.93	4.39	4.98	5.02
Household working members	69.4%	63.1%	67.5%	85.3%	85.7%	91.4%	61.3%	59.1%	52.3%	67.5%	62.7%	62.1%
Motivation for starting												
By necessity	6.9%	11.0%	7.7%	25.0%	29.5%	19.3%	n.a	n.a	n.a	34.8%	53.6%	50.4%
By choice	76.6%	73.2%	66.9%	49.3%	55.0%	59.2%	n.a	n.a	n.a	50.0%	38.0%	41.9%
By tradition	16.5%	15.7%	25.4%	9.7%	12.5%	17.9%	n.a	n.a	n.a	15.2%	6.0%	7.7%
Branch												
Manufacture	26.4%	25.3%	31.5%	37.4%	32.8%	48.7%	22.1%	18.4%	20.4%	32.4%	8.3%	13.4%
Trade	38.5%	20.8%	21.9%	35.6%	44.4%	31.6%	45.5%	0.5%	46.0%	13.7%	24.2%	34.1%
Services	35.1%	54.0%	46.6%	27.0%	22.9%	19.7%	32.4%	0.3%	33.6%	54.0%	67.5%	52.6%

Table A.1. **Main individual, household and business characteristics of young entrepreneurs by performance level** (*cont.*)

	Viet Nam			Madagascar			Côte d'Ivoire			Peru		
	Top	Middle	Low	Top	Middle	Low	Top	Middle	Low	Top	Middle	Low
Premises												
Outside	8.6%	23.2%	18.0%	31.7%	52.5%	50.1%	59.4%	66.2%	64.5%	22.1%	59.2%	51.8%
Home	56.7%	38.5%	48.5%	11.9%	26.2%	29.4%	21.1%	23.6%	24.9%	30.6%	26.1%	35.2%
Dedicated	34.7%	38.3%	33.6%	56.3%	19.7%	18.8%	19.5%	9.7%	9.5%	47.3%	12.3%	11.5%
Infrastructure and ICT												
Water	26.6%	21.0%	23.0%	30.1%	9.6%	8.9%	n.a	n.a	n.a	33.8%	7.8%	9.0%
Electricity	60.6%	67.6%	70.8%	18.4%	6.4%	5.4%	n.a	n.a	n.a	61.2%	23.0%	23.6%
Phone	84.0%	52.2%	47.3%	22.1%	7.5%	6.3%	n.a	n.a	n.a	14.1%	1.8%	2.2%
Internet	17.2%	15.7%	16.2%	0.0%	0.1%	0.1%	n.a	n.a	n.a	17.7%	2.8%	3.0%
Unregistered businesses	64.7%	75.3%	89.0%	93.7%	95.9%	97.7%	94.0%	98.7%	99.3%	48.0%	89.1%	95.6%
Bookkeeping (written accounts)	68.1%	36.6%	22.2%	37.1%	12.1%	5.9%	42.6%	32.3%	28.9%	59.2%	22.4%	22.1%
Business strategies												
Prospect customers	27.5%	38.2%	28.6%	10.2%	24.1%	23.1%	n.a	n.a	n.a	n.a	n.a	n.a
Change suppliers to reduce cost	23.9%	22.5%	22.2%	15.4%	2.3%	2.6%	n.a	n.a	n.a	n.a	n.a	n.a
Move to less costly premises	0.0%	1.2%	0.9%	2.5%	2.3%	2.1%	n.a	n.a	n.a	n.a	n.a	n.a
Limit manpower costs	12.5%	1.3%	1.6%	5.0%	0.2%	0.4%	n.a	n.a	n.a	n.a	n.a	n.a
At least one strategy	42.6%	47.5%	39.3%	33.1%	28.9%	28.2%	n.a	n.a	n.a	n.a	n.a	n.a
Innovation (either products/services or processes)	11.3%	8.4%	20.0%	n.a	n.a	n.a	n.a	n.a	n.a	n.a	n.a	n.a
Employment												
Number of workers	3.90	1.54	1.63	3.36	1.26	1.16	3.81	1.52	1.39	3.04	1.19	1.15
Businesses that created jobs	100.0%	9.5%	20.8%	100.0%	3.5%	5.0%	100.0%	13.8%	21.5%	n.a	n.a	n.a

Source: Côte d'Ivoire ENSETE 2014, Madagascar ENEMPSI 2012, Peru ENAHO 2014, and Viet Nam LFS and HBIS 2014.

Table A.2. Marginal effects on the probability of belonging to different youth entrepreneurial performance levels

		Viet Nam		Madagascar		Côte d'Ivoire		Peru		Overall	
Dedicated premises	Top	0.00	(2.03)*	0.02	(-1.88)	0.04	(42.39)**	0.05	(92.56)**	0.03	(79.61)**
	Middle	0.12	(96.91)**	0.07	(-1.91)	0.05	(23.42)**	0.17	(84.14)**	0.09	(117.40)**
	Low	-0.12	(105.09)**	-0.10	(2.54)*	-0.09	(41.86)**	-0.22	(108.58)**	-0.12	(155.22)**
Informal	Top	-0.02	(24.85)**	-0.04	(-1.75)	-0.08	(46.10)**	-0.04	(86.06)**	-0.05	(130.96)**
	Middle	-0.09	(60.71)**	-1.57	(14.06)**	-0.13	(21.88)**	-0.11	(50.73)**	-0.11	(99.44)**
	Low	0.11	(77.45)**	1.61	(14.39)**	0.21	(33.24)**	0.15	(71.00)**	0.16	(143.99)**
Branch: Trade	Top	0.00	(4.63)**	-0.01	(-1.07)	-0.01	(17.09)**	-0.07	(102.37)**	-0.02	(55.04)**
	Middle	-0.03	(18.28)**	0.06	(2.18)*	0.05	(30.32)**	0.10	(58.41)**	0.07	(85.94)**
	Low	0.03	(18.21)**	-0.05	(-1.88)	-0.03	(22.17)**	-0.03	(19.63)**	-0.05	(63.81)**
Branch: Services	Top	-0.06	(59.26)**	-0.02	(-1.41)	-0.01	(9.29)**	-0.05	(97.19)**	-0.03	(77.82)**
	Middle	0.07	(40.58)**	0.04	(-1.13)	0.02	(11.07)**	0.07	(44.60)**	0.08	(107.99)**
	Low	0.00	(2.09)*	-0.02	(-0.54)	-0.01	(6.41)**	-0.02	(13.13)**	-0.05	(73.44)**
Access to water	Top	0.06	(60.96)**	0.01	(-0.63)	n.a.		0.02	(37.76)**	n.a	
	Middle	0.01	(6.39)**	-0.01	(-0.14)	n.a.		-0.03	(15.32)**	n.a	
	Low	-0.06	(51.47)**	0.00	(-0.06)	n.a.		0.01	(4.60)**	n.a	
Access to electricity	Top	-0.06	(81.08)**	0.00	(-0.09)	n.a.		0.00	(4.77)**	n.a	
	Middle	0.00	(2.29)*	0.03	(-0.63)	n.a.		0.04	(24.25)**	n.a	
	Low	0.06	(54.76)**	-0.03	(-0.63)	n.a.		-0.03	(23.35)**	n.a	
Access to phone	Top	0.09	(117.73)**	0.00	(-0.1)	n.a.		0.01	(8.25)**	n.a	
	Middle	0.11	(80.97)**	0.16	(2.44)*	n.a.		-0.08	(17.39)**	n.a	
	Low	-0.19	(165.73)**	-0.16	(2.43)*	n.a.		0.08	(16.17)**	n.a	
Access to Internet	Top	-0.01	(11.25)**	-0.29	(4.78)**	n.a.		0.04	(58.80)**	n.a	
	Middle	-0.08	(57.47)**	1.86	(9.94)**	n.a.		0.07	(14.94)**	n.a	
	Low	0.09	(73.35)**	-1.57	(9.45)**	n.a.		-0.11	(23.47)**	n.a	
Male	Top	-0.01	(12.56)**	0.01	(-1.46)	0.06	(92.95)**	0.04	(83.54)**	0.03	(112.87)**
	Middle	0.17	(164.89)**	0.10	(4.08)**	0.02	(12.93)**	0.27	(275.81)**	0.18	(330.05)**
	Low	-0.16	(179.18)**	-0.12	(4.92)**	-0.08	(67.32)**	-0.31	(347.10)**	-0.22	(413.55)**
Education: upper secondary	Top	0.09	(62.76)**	0.03	(2.01)*	-0.01	(7.89)**	0.05	(33.16)**	0.02	(67.00)**
	Middle	-0.08	(50.70)**	0.04	(-1.43)	-0.03	(19.68)**	-0.03	(14.76)**	-0.03	(38.02)**
	Low	-0.01	(8.42)**	-0.06	(2.91)**	0.03	(25.34)**	-0.02	(14.29)**	0.01	(7.73)**
Education: college or tertiary	Top	0.09	(63.05)**	0.03	(-1.43)	0.01	(3.39)**	0.04	(24.44)**	0.02	(55.32)**
	Middle	-0.09	(52.40)**	0.04	(-0.63)	0.04	(12.03)**	-0.07	(33.91)**	-0.04	(45.16)**
	Low	0.01	(3.35)**	-0.07	(-1.14)	-0.04	(13.92)**	0.03	(19.22)**	0.02	(20.46)**
Ethnic	Top	0.02	(26.68)**	n.a.		n.a.		n.a.		n.a	
	Middle	-0.06	(36.24)**	n.a.		n.a.		n.a.		n.a	
	Low	0.04	(25.38)**	n.a.		n.a.		n.a.		n.a	
Urban	Top	0.04	(68.55)**	0.01	(-1.03)	0.04	(54.62)**	0.02	(23.66)**	0.03	(92.67)**
	Middle	0.05	(49.65)**	0.11	(4.31)**	0.00	(2.76)**	0.15	(108.10)**	0.08	(119.11)**
	Low	-0.10	(94.93)**	-0.12	(5.46)**	-0.04	(34.32)**	-0.17	(136.98)**	-0.11	(178.70)**

Table A.2. Marginal effects on the probability of belonging to different youth entrepreneurial performance levels *(cont.)*

		Viet Nam		Madagascar		Côte d'Ivoire		Peru		Overall	
Motivation: by necessity	Top	-0.05	(55.34)**	0.01	(-1.5)	n.a.		0.00	(8.99)**	n.a	
	Middle	0.05	(30.05)**	0.04	(-1.56)	n.a.		0.07	(68.01)**	n.a	
	Low	0.00	(-0.23)	-0.05	(2.21)*	n.a.		-0.06	(68.19)**	n.a	
Has a strategy	Top	-0.03	(45.06)**	0.00	(-0.18)	n.a.		n.a.		n.a	
	Middle	0.24	(211.32)**	-0.02	(-0.66)	n.a.		n.a.		n.a	
	Low	-0.21	(201.46)**	0.01	(-0.64)	n.a.		n.a.		n.a	
Proactivity	Top	n.a.		0.00	(-0.12)	n.a.		n.a.		n.a	
	Middle	n.a.		-0.02	(-0.75)	n.a.		n.a.		n.a	
	Low	n.a.		0.02	(-0.89)	n.a.		n.a.		n.a	
Reaction to shocks	Top	n.a.		0.02	(-1.44)	n.a.		n.a.		n.a	
	Middle	n.a.		-0.03	(-0.8)	n.a.		n.a.		n.a	
	Low	n.a.		0.01	(-0.31)	n.a.		n.a.		n.a	
Active pricing	Top	n.a.		0.01	(-0.86)	n.a.		n.a.		n.a	
	Middle	n.a.		0.01	(-0.3)	n.a.		n.a.		n.a	
	Low	n.a.		-0.02	(-0.68)	n.a.		n.a.		n.a	
Innovation	Top	-0.03	(25.80)**	n.a.		n.a.		n.a.		n.a	
	Middle	-0.31	(137.81)**	n.a.		n.a.		n.a.		n.a	
	Low	0.34	(160.84)**	n.a.		n.a.		n.a.		n.a	
Written accounts	Top	0.06	(96.28)**	0.03	(2.74)**	0.03	(37.98)**	0.03	(67.13)**	0.05	(176.04)**
	Middle	-0.04	(29.20)**	-0.01	(-0.34)	0.01	(4.06)**	0.02	(18.25)**	0.02	(36.96)**
	Low	-0.02	(18.78)**	-0.01	(-0.4)	-0.03	(25.72)**	-0.05	(44.92)**	-0.07	(117.24)**
Observations		891 998		-		759 191		934 677		3 002 873	
Observations (unweighted)		239		1 162		1 757		3 030		6 226	

Note: Marginal effects obtained from multinomial regression models. Statistical significance: *10%, **5%, ***1%.
Source: Côte d'Ivoire ENSETE 2014, Madagascar ENEMPSI 2012, Peru ENAHO 2014, and Viet Nam LFS and HBIS 2014.

Table A.3. Young entrepreneurs express problems, by entrepreneurial performance level

	Viet Nam (in %)			Madagascar (in %)		
	Top	Middle	Low	Top	Middle	Low
In selling your production	45.7	26.3	44.0	56.8	47.7	47.2
In accessing credit	7.3	17.9	29.1	76.7	47.7	41.1
Lacking space, access to land, inadequate premises	19.6	22.7	32.2	15.9	14.3	11.0
Because of machine or equipment	34.0	10.0	26.1	25.4	22.0	29.1
Regulatory burden, registration, taxes				7.6	3.1	0.3
Because of corruption	2.3	1.7	13.9	n.a	n.a	n.a
Because of transportation	17.3	7.3	16.0	n.a	n.a	n.a
Because of inflation	41.3	11.8	36.1	n.a	n.a	n.a
Because of crime, theft and disorder	18.1	5.3	25.2	n.a	n.a	n.a
Because of health issues	20.3	7.9	30.5	n.a	n.a	n.a

Source: Madagascar ENEMPSI 2012, and Viet Nam HBIS 2014.

Table A.4. Young entrepreneurs express assistance needs, by entrepreneurial performance level

	Viet Nam (%)			Madagascar (%)		
	Top	Middle	Low	Top	Middle	Low
Technical training	18.3	17.8	41.6	37.6	25.5	29.9
Training in organisation and accounts	11.1	5.7	10.7	21.2	24.1	17.3
Assistance for supply of raw materials	40.2	15.7	36.9	27.2	36.5	37.3
Access to modern machines	53.0	26.0	31.9	22.1	27.8	35.2
Access to loan	46.4	46.8	44.5	27.1	23.6	17.5
Access to information on the market	59.7	37.0	30.1	29.0	25.4	20.4
Access to big orders	64.7	37.2	45.1	37.0	46.3	42.8
Registration of your business	0.0	12.8	23.0	17.7	18.3	15.2
Advertising for your new products/services	24.4	13.2	27.2	28.4	17.3	14.1

Source: Madagascar ENEMPSI 2012, and Viet Nam HBIS 2014.

Table A.5. Young entrepreneurs express problems upon business inception, by entrepreneurial performance level

	Côte d'Ivoire (%)		
	Top	Middle	Low
None	38.0	36.3	42.2
Capital/credit	47.7	54.0	45.7
Skills	2.7	2.0	3.5
Legal framework	1.9	0.7	0.5
Workspace	6.6	5.5	4.8
Other	3.0	1.5	3.4

Source: Côte d'Ivoire ENSETE 2014.

ORGANISATION FOR ECONOMIC CO-OPERATION AND DEVELOPMENT

The OECD is a unique forum where governments work together to address the economic, social and environmental challenges of globalisation. The OECD is also at the forefront of efforts to understand and to help governments respond to new developments and concerns, such as corporate governance, the information economy and the challenges of an ageing population. The Organisation provides a setting where governments can compare policy experiences, seek answers to common problems, identify good practice and work to co-ordinate domestic and international policies.

The OECD member countries are: Australia, Austria, Belgium, Canada, Chile, the Czech Republic, Denmark, Estonia, Finland, France, Germany, Greece, Hungary, Iceland, Ireland, Israel, Italy, Japan, Korea, Latvia, Luxembourg, Mexico, the Netherlands, New Zealand, Norway, Poland, Portugal, the Slovak Republic, Slovenia, Spain, Sweden, Switzerland, Turkey, the United Kingdom and the United States. The European Union takes part in the work of the OECD.

OECD Publishing disseminates widely the results of the Organisation's statistics gathering and research on economic, social and environmental issues, as well as the conventions, guidelines and standards agreed by its members.

OECD DEVELOPMENT CENTRE

The OECD Development Centre was established in 1962 as an independent platform for knowledge sharing and policy dialogue between OECD member countries and developing economies, allowing these countries to interact on an equal footing. Today, 27 OECD countries and 25 non-OECD countries are members of the Centre. The Centre draws attention to emerging systemic issues likely to have an impact on global development and more specific development challenges faced by today's developing and emerging economies. It uses evidence-based analysis and strategic partnerships to help countries formulate innovative policy solutions to the global challenges of development.

For more information on the Centre and its members, please see *www.oecd.org/dev*.

OECD PUBLISHING, 2, rue André-Pascal, 75775 PARIS CEDEX 16
(41 2017 16 1 P) ISBN 978-92-64-27782-3 – 2017

www.ingramcontent.com/pod-product-compliance
Lightning Source LLC
Chambersburg PA
CBHW080639280726
48659CB00025BA/2638